THE BATTLE OF MALDON
AND
OTHER OLD ENGLISH POEMS

Also by
Kevin Crossley-Holland

ON APPROVAL (poems)
HAVELOK THE DANE
KING HORN

Also by
Bruce Mitchell

A GUIDE TO OLD ENGLISH

The Battle of Maldon
and
Other Old English Poems

Translated by
KEVIN CROSSLEY-HOLLAND
and Edited by
BRUCE MITCHELL

MACMILLAN
London · Melbourne · Toronto

ST MARTIN'S PRESS
New York
1966

Copyright © Kevin Crossley-Holland and Bruce Mitchell 1965

First Edition 1965
Reprinted 1966

MACMILLAN AND COMPANY LIMITED
Little Essex Street London WC 2
also Bombay Calcutta Madras Melbourne

THE MACMILLAN COMPANY OF CANADA LIMITED
70 Bond Street Toronto 2

ST MARTIN'S PRESS INC
175 Fifth Avenue New York NY 10010

Library of Congress Catalog card no. 65–13048

PRINTED IN GREAT BRITAIN

For
Caroline and Mollie

ACKNOWLEDGEMENTS ARE DUE

To the editors of the *Listener* and the *Spectator* in which a number of these translations have appeared; to the B.B.C. Third Programme in which many of these translations have been broadcast; for the use of seven riddles, reprinted from *A Knot of Riddles* by Sir Arthur Bliss by permission of Novello & Co. Ltd.; to Basil Blackwell, the publishers, for permission to reprint a section from Bruce Mitchell's *A Guide to Old English*; and, finally, to the author, publishers, and editors of those books and journals from which quotations have been made in this book.

CONTENTS

TRANSLATOR'S NOTE

I SHOULD like to express my thanks both to my father and to Dr. Edward Lowbury for their generous encouragement and assistance; to Mario Rinvolucri, whose insight and unsparing criticism helped to shape these translations; and to the editor, upon whose knowledge and understanding of the texts I often called, to work with whom has been a very great pleasure.

KEVIN CROSSLEY-HOLLAND

EDITOR'S NOTE

THE debt I owe to the many scholars who have written on Old English literature is readily apparent. The one I owe to my pupils is less so. But both are gratefully acknowledged.

A few people must be mentioned by name. I am grateful for help on various problems to The Rev. N. L. A. Tidwell, St. Stephen's House, Oxford, The Rev. H. E. J. Cowdrey and Dr. R. Fargher, both of St. Edmund Hall, Oxford. The Rev. Graham Midgley, of St. Edmund Hall, read through my work and made some much-appreciated suggestions. J. L. Smith, of St. Edmund Hall, gave valuable help with the proofs. My association with the translator has been a happy one, and the debt we both owe to our wives is acknowledged with gratitude in the dedication.

To Professor A. Campbell, Professor C. L. Wrenn, and Professor J. R. R. Tolkien (all of Oxford), I owe more than I can say. Had I not sat at their feet, I could not have shared in producing this book. That they will not find it totally unworthy is my hope.

BRUCE MITCHELL

GENERAL INTRODUCTION

I. Manuscripts Containing Old English Poetry

Most of the Old English poetry which has escaped the ravages of time and the attentions of such destructive agencies as rats and mice, fire, and Christians zealous to extirpate the works of paganism, is to be found in four great manuscripts or codices — the Junius Manuscript, the Vercelli Book, the Exeter Book, and the *Beowulf* Manuscript (Volumes I–IV respectively of the Columbia *Anglo-Saxon Poetic Records*). All these date from the second half of the tenth century. So also does our chief source for the Old English version of the *Metres of Boethius*, traditionally ascribed to King Alfred; they are based on the earlier prose translation of Boethius's *De Consolatione Philosophiae* and bear no direct relationship to the Latin text. They are, however, of no great interest to us and are not represented in this book. Along with them in Volume V of *The Anglo-Saxon Poetic Records* will be found the metrical versions of Psalms 51–150 which survive in the Paris Psalter. This translation was perhaps made in the late ninth or early tenth century. It too is not represented here, for it is of little poetic value, its author having been variously characterized as a 'careless and uninventive scribe' and as a 'crude worker'. The remaining poems — those which have survived in other manuscripts or in later transcripts of manuscripts now lost — have been collected in Volume VI of *The Anglo-Saxon Poetic Records*.

The Junius Manuscript — Junius 11 of the Bodleian Library, Oxford — is so named after the Dutch scholar Junius, who in 1655 published an edition of it in Amsterdam, in which he described the poems as the work of the monk Cædmon; indeed the manuscript is now sometimes known as the Cædmon Manuscript, because of the extraordinary similarity of its contents to the list of works attributed by Bede to Cædmon. After Cædmon had been inspired to sing his famous Hymn —

I

thereby (some say) first using the pagan Germanic verse forms for Christian purposes — he went on (we are told) to paraphrase portions of Holy Scripture in verse. The Junius Manuscript contains a paraphrase of part of the book of *Genesis*, a striking poem called *Exodus*, the story of Daniel, and a poem known as *Christ and Satan* which contains a lament of the fallen angels, the life of Christ from the Crucifixion to the Last Judgement, and an account of His Temptation. These are very like the passages Cædmon is said to have paraphrased. But the subjects were not copyright and the differences in style are such that the same man could not be the author of all the poems in the Junius Manuscript. Nevertheless, if we accept that Cædmon first sang Christian stories in alliterative verse, we can think of him as their inspirer.

Interestingly enough, this manuscript is also linked with another great Christian poet, John Milton. The poem known as *Genesis* contains two parts — one a fairly lifeless paraphrase of *Genesis* up to the sacrifice of Isaac and the other an interpolation which gives a lively account of the Fall of the Angels and the Temptation of Adam and Eve. The latter is now known to be a ninth-century translation from Old Saxon. In this, Satan is a defiant heroic figure similar to Milton's Satan and far removed from the elegiac Satan who laments the loss of the glories of Heaven. Milton appears to have known Junius. But, tempting as it is to believe that the Old English poem influenced his conception of Satan, it is at best an unproven hypothesis; what correspondences there are can be attributed to the similarity of the subject and to independent poetic inspiration.

None of the poems in the Junius Manuscript are presented here in full, but extracts from *Genesis B* and *Exodus* are given later in this Introduction.

The Vercelli Book or *Codex Vercellensis* lies in the chapter library of the cathedral at Vercelli in northern Italy. How it got there is not known. On the evidence of a marginal jotting, Dr. Kenneth Sisam has shown that there is strong reason for believing that it was already in northern Italy in the eleventh century. He thus eliminates certain attractive ways of accounting for its presence in Italy, and finds no justification for choosing one rather than another of those travellers who might have carried it to Vercelli in the eleventh century. But he goes on:

There is something unattractive about an argument which leaves bare ground where before there was a rich crop of interesting hypotheses; so I shall attempt a purely conjectural reconstruction.

At some time in the first half of the eleventh century an eminent Englishman decided to make the journey to Rome. To and fro, it was a journey of months, with many hours of rest or waiting on the weather, which good reading for himself and his company would help to pass. As its head or patron, he was able to borrow from the library of a monastic church, and the choice fell on the Vercelli Book. It is essentially a reading-book: there is nothing in it that would support a claim at Rome, or help in a controversy on liturgy or doctrine; and whoever chose it had old-fashioned tastes, for it is an out-of-the-way collection. It includes nothing by the new popular sermon-writers Ælfric and Wulfstan; and in a period from which many collections survive, it is the only manuscript for about half its sermons. Crossing by the Great St. Bernard, the party halted at Vercelli. At the cathedral service there, the leader (if he was an ecclesiastic) or an attendant priest skilled in music, heard the *capitellum* 'Adiutor meus esto' sung with a text, division, and melody strikingly different from the English use, and noted it, or perhaps asked an Italian to write it, in a convenient place — the first blank space in the English sermon-book. At this stage it was intended to bring the manuscript home again; but some chance intervened. Possibly one of the party stayed behind sick at Vercelli, and the book was left to comfort him. Possibly on the outward journey it was left for safe keeping in the cathedral, to be picked up on the return, which some change of plan, such as a diversion via Mont Cenis, prevented. Possibly when the loads were made up to recross the Alps, something had to be sacrificed, a new treasure was preferred to the old book, and conscience was salved by leaving it to the cathedral. Such commonplace reasons, which no chronicle or document is likely to record, would account for its remaining with the books of Vercelli Cathedral.

The six poems of the Vercelli Book all deal with religious subjects. Two — *Andreas* and *Elene* — tell of the lives of saints. The remaining four are shorter poems. Of them, only *The Dream of the Rood* is translated here.

The Exeter Book, the largest of the four great collections of Old English poetry, can be seen in the library of Exeter Cathedral. It is generally agreed that it is the *mycel englisc boc* 'the big English book' given to the cathedral by Leofric, the first bishop of Exeter, who died in 1072. Many of the poems it contains deal with religious subjects. The first poem, known as *Christ*, was divided by Professor Cook into three sections which he called respectively 'The Advent', 'The Ascension', and 'The Last Judgement' or 'Doomsday'. The second tells the story of St. Guthlac. The third *Azarias* tells part of the story of *Daniel*. The fourth is a religious allegory called *The Phoenix*. But there are poems on other than religious subjects, including some fine lyrics and elegies, and the *Riddles*. The poems from the Exeter Book translated here are: *The Wanderer, The Seafarer, The Panther, The Whale, Deor, Wulf,* a selection of the *Riddles, The Wife's Lament, The Husband's Message,* and *The Ruin*.

The *Beowulf* Manuscript — the British Museum Cotton Vitellius A. xv — was damaged, but fortunately not destroyed, by the fire which in 1731 swept through the Cottonian collection of manuscripts. A few words were lost from many pages and some damage was done by crumbling of the burnt edges before the folios were remounted and rebound, perhaps some time in the 1860s. The most badly damaged parts of the manuscript were those containing *Beowulf*. Again fortunately, we have the two Thorkelin transcripts of *Beowulf* made in 1786–7, one by an unknown copyist, the other by the Icelander Thorkelin, the first editor of the poem. The manuscript also contains a 350 line fragment of the poem *Judith* (a Jewish 'saint's life' based on the Vulgate story) and some prose texts. The most interesting of these are perhaps those known as *The Wonders of the East* and *Alexander's Letter to Aristotle*, which (in the words of Renwick and Orton) show 'that long before the Conquest the Anglo-Saxons found entertainment in the exotic romanticism of the East'.

The Metres of Boethius and the metrical psalms of *The Paris Psalter* need no further comment. Of the poems from miscellaneous sources, those translated here are *The Battle of Maldon*, *The Battle of Brunanburh*, *The Finnesburh Fragment*, some of the *Charms*, *Cædmon's Hymn*, and the inscription on the Brussels Cross. For further remarks on these, see the comments which precede the appropriate translation.

II. WHAT TYPES OF POETRY SURVIVE?

A rough classification by subject matter is attempted here. The poems asterisked are included in this book.

Poems treating heroic subjects:

Beowulf, *Deor, *The Finnesburh Fragment, *Waldere*, *Widsith*.

Historical poems:

*The Battle of Brunanburh, *The Battle of Maldon.

Biblical paraphrases and re-workings of biblical subjects:

The Metrical Psalms, The poems of the Junius Manuscript, *Christ*, *Azarias*, and *Judith*.

Lives of the Saints:

Andreas, *Elene*, *Guthlac*, *Juliana*.

Other religious poems:

There are many shorter religious poems. Among them *The Dream of the Rood and the allegorical poems — *The Phoenix*, *The Panther and *The Whale — should be noted.

B

Short Elegies and Lyrics:

*The Wife's Lament, *The Husband's Message, *The Ruin, *The Wanderer, *The Seafarer, *Wulf. *Deor too could be included here.

Riddles and Gnomic Verses:

A selection from the *Riddles is included in this book. Gnomic verses or Maxims (as they are sometimes called) are to be found in the Exeter Book and in the MS. Cotton Tiberius B.i, which also contains one of the texts of the Anglo-Saxon Chronicle. These contain a variety of proverbs and gnomes which blend Christian and pagan ideas. A brief specimen from the Exeter Book is translated here:

> God does not stand guard over a man
> Unreliable or reckless,
> Subversive or untrue.
> Long ago the Lord created many things, commanding them
>   to exist for ever.
> Wise words are appropriate for every man,
> A song for the minstrel, good sense for other men.
> Every man in the world has his own mind
> And, in his mind, his own longings.
> Yet he who can sing numerous songs
> Or pluck the harp with his hands longs the less,
> For he has the gift of music, given by God.
> Unhappy the man who must live alone;
> Fate has ordained that he shall be friendless.
> He would be better off with a brother
> (Both sons of one warrior), should they attack a wild boar
> Or a bear — that beast with cruel paws.
> Those warriors shall always shoulder their armour
> Side by side together and together take their rest;
> No man shall separate them,
> Death only will divide them.
> The two shall sit and play dice while their grief departs,
> Forget the harshness of fate while they play at the board.

Miscellaneous:

The Charms (represented here in part), *The Runic Poem*, *The Riming Poem*.

III. The Poems Here Translated

The selection of the poems to be translated here (those asterisked in the preceding section) has been based on two criteria — they must be short enough to be presented in their entirety and they must be worth presenting in their own right, either as poems or (in a few cases) because they are interesting historically or by virtue of their contents. The arrangement is not chronological, but moves from the battle poems which throw light on the pagan heroic code, through the poems which deal with the more personal and intimate side of the life of the pagan Anglo-Saxons, to those which deal with Christian themes, culminating in the greatest of the shorter Old English poems *The Dream of the Rood*. Each translation is prefaced by a brief editorial note.

IV. The Poems Not Translated Here

The most interesting of these are perhaps *Genesis B*, *Exodus*, *Judith*, and *Beowulf*. *Genesis B* is the name given to the translation from Old Saxon already mentioned. Its 617 lines give us a Miltonic Satan whose fall is the result of *ofermod* 'over-mood', the quality of too much pride which we shall meet in *The Battle of Maldon*. The few lines which follow are the thoughts of Satan before his fall. They give us a glimpse of the powers of the Old Saxon poet and provide an interesting comparison with *Paradise Lost*:

Our Lord loved him dearly; yet it could not be disguised
    from Him
That His angel had become bloated with pride,
Had rebelled against his master, making boastful claims
In a most hostile manner and would not obey Him:

He said that he was strikingly handsome,
Gleaming white, irradiant; he announced that he could not
    find it
In his heart to humble himself by serving God, by following
The Lord with loyalty; he said it seemed to him
That he had strength and skills
Such as Holy God, with his companions in war,
Would never have. The angel boasted
About many things, and planned how he, through his own
    power,
Would establish a mightier throne for himself,
Higher in heaven; he said that his heart
Urged him to erect buildings in the north
And in the west; he declared it seemed doubtful
Whether he would remain as God's disciple:
'Why should I sweat?' said he. 'I need
No master; I can work as many wonders
With my own hands; I have such strength
That I'll establish a greater throne,
Higher in heaven. Why should I crave His favours
And bow and scrape before Him? I can be God as well as He.
Staunch comrades stand by me, strong-minded warriors
Who'll not fail me in the fight; fearless men have elected me
As their leader; with support from such warlike companions
One may devise and execute a plan. My friends are eager
And loyal in their hearts; I can be their lord
And rule in this kingdom. Thus it would appear
That I have no reason whatsoever to flatter God;
I will no longer be His follower.'

Exodus, which tells the story of the journey of the Children
of Israel to the Promised Land, with particular emphasis on
the escape from Pharaoh's army at the Red Sea, is one of the
more successful religious epics. Here, as in *Judith*, the heroic
and biblical blend happily, perhaps because in both cases the
biblical stories are about 'heroic' peoples. Its warlike atmo-
sphere, the drowning of the Egyptians in the Red Sea, and the
grim exultation of the Hebrews, make the subject a 'natural'
for the Old English poet, who atones for his lack of char-

acterization by his dramatic power, descriptive ability, bold imagery, and daring use of words. At times he is too excited; Professor Tolkien once remarked in a lecture 'At the Red Sea, he just foams. . . .' The passage which follows exemplifies this:

> The Egyptians were terrified; the torrents of water
> Filled them with fear, the flood threatened their lives.
> The mountainous rollers were crested with blood,
> The sea flung up gore, the waves were in uproar,
> Weapons littered the water, a death-mist rose from the sea.
> The Egyptians were forced to retrace their footsteps;
> In terror they fled, stricken with panic. Fearful
> Of the conflict, they longed for the safety of their own homes;
> Their boasting was less confident. Wave after wave, rolling
>   relentlessly,
> Cast dark shadows over them; out of that army not one man
> Returned home, but the fateful waves cut them off
> From behind; where, before, the road had run across the sand,
> The sea was spuming; the soldiers were engulfed.
> The waves reared up, the storm and the shrieks
> Of the army soared towards Heaven;
> The enemy cried out in despair, the air above grew dark
> With their doomed voices; water mingled with blood.
> The defensive sea-wall was dashed to the ground; the sky
>   was lashed
> With the sounds of thousands drowning; brave men died,
> Kings surrounded by their dead bodyguards; there, at the
>   sea's edge,
> All hope of safety was snatched away; the shields shone.
> The water-wall, the raging sea, rose
> High over the warriors' heads; the whole army was clasped
> In death's embrace, deprived of the means of escape,
> Every warrior weighed down by his armour.

However, the poem is more than just a narrative; it is also allegorical. The journey of the Children of Israel is at the same time man's journey through life. The enemy is both Pharaoh and the Devil. By virtue of this simultaneity, the poet generally succeeds in avoiding the dull didactic tone into which some

Old English poets fall. As E. B. Irving, Jr., the latest editor of
Exodus, tells us, 'the author of *Exodus* was a true poet . . . he
has heightened and enhanced the spiritual significance of his
theme, and to the power inherent in that story he has infused
creatively the vigor of his own idiom and poetic tradition'.

Judith was very highly praised by Henry Sweet. 'Of this
poem,' he wrote, 'only the last three cantos have been pre-
served. Enough, however, is left to show that the complete
work must have been one of the noblest in the whole range of
Old English poetry.' This high praise is not undeserved. The
poem is in some ways conventional. It owes much to the
religious epic in phrasing and outlook. Judith's fierce purity
recalls that of St. Juliana, though to be sure the former slew
her would-be ravisher — 'she fiercely struck the heathen dog
so that his head rolled to the floor' — while the latter suffered
torture and death rather than share an honourable marriage-
bed with a pagan prince who would not become a Christian.
But the poet gives us a clear insight into the characters of
Holofernes and Judith, much realistic detail in description,
and touches of the grimly-ironical humour which we find in
Byrhtnoth's first speech in *The Battle of Maldon*. Some of these
characteristics can be seen in the following splendid passage
which describes the morning after a great feast. Holofernes is
still within the tent to which, in his drunken lust, he had taken
Judith. But now it is morning, and, unknown to the Assyrian
warriors, Judith has killed Holofernes and taken his head in
a bag back to the Jewish stronghold of Bethulia. There she has
hastily organized an attack on the Assyrian camp, and the sur-
prised warriors rush to warn their leader. The poet continues:

> . . . Then I heard
> That the doomed warriors woke immediately,
> That crowds of cheerless men
> Pressed towards the pavilion
> Of evil Holofernes, anxious to alert
> Their lord to the threat of battle
> Before the full might of the Hebrew host
> Should descend upon them. They all imagined

That the beautiful maiden and the leader of men —
Judith the pure and the lecherous prince,
Savage and intolerant — were asleep together
In the fine tent; but not one of those earls
Dared awaken the warrior,
Discover how his prince
Had fared with the holy maid,
The virgin of the Lord. The Hebrew troop
Advanced, fighting ferociously
With their sharp swords; with bloodstained weapons
They paid off old insults,
Former debts; during that day
Assyrian glory was ground into the dust,
Assyrian pride was humbled. The men stood
Round their lord's tent, exceedingly excited
And troubled in mind. Then all together
They began to cough and hum and haw
And gnash their teeth (without God on their side
They groaned in despair); then their glory,
Their courage and prosperity, were at an end. The earls
    attempted
To wake their lord without the slightest success.
At last one of the warriors
Took his courage in both hands and stepped
Into the pavilion; their peril constrained him.
Then he saw his gold-giver stretched on the bed,
Ashen of hue, deprived of life's breath,
Dead. At once he collapsed
Onto the ground, distraught and numbed;
He tore out his hair and tore his clothes too,
And shouted these words to the warriors
Who stood outside, still waiting anxiously:
'Here, in our lord's death, is our own end discovered
And seen to be at hand; the time
Draws near — because of this deed —
When we must lose our lives together,
Perish in battle; here lies our leader,
Headless, hewn by the sword.' Then, sick at heart,
They threw away their weapons
And, despairing, sought safety in flight.

Of *Beowulf* little need be said here. A recent critic has announced that he still unhesitatingly rejects 'the idea that *Beowulf* can conceivably be regarded as a source of pleasure by anyone above the cultural level of a retarded ceorl'. Let him speak for himself. The fact remains that many regard *Beowulf* as fit to rank among the greatest poems of our language and, in this nuclear age when the monsters and dragons seem closer to us and the powers of darkness seem to be in the ascendant, find that they can derive comfort and encouragement from it. It is fitting that the last word on it here should be Professor Tolkien's, for he more than anyone else has brought about the recognition of *Beowulf*'s true stature:

There is not much poetry in the world like this; and though *Beowulf* may not be among the very greatest poems of our western world and its tradition, it has its own individual character, and peculiar solemnity; it would still have power had it been written in some time or place unknown and without posterity, if it contained no name that could now be recognized or identified by research. Yet it is in fact written in a language that after many centuries has still essential kinship with our own, it was made in this land, and moves in our northern world beneath our northern sky, and for those who are native to that tongue and land, it must ever call with a profound appeal — until the dragon comes.

V. What We Learn of the Anglo-Saxons from their Literature

The Germanic tribes who settled in England in the fifth century brought with them the Germanic heroic code. What we can discover about it from Old English literature generally confirms the observations of Tacitus in his *Germania*. The salient points are these. The Germanic warrior was a member of a *comitatus*, a warrior-band. Life was a struggle against insuperable odds, against the inevitable doom decreed by a meaningless fate — *Wyrd*, which originally meant 'what happens'. There is no evidence in their literature that the pagan Anglo-Saxons believed in a life after death like that of Valhalla, the hall in Scandinavian mythology reserved for dead heroes, though there are references to the worship of heathen gods such as Woden, and the practice of burying coins, weapons, and other goods, with the dead, suggests a belief in some kind of after-life where they could be used. It is, however, a different kind of immortality which is stressed in their literature. This was *lof*, which was won by bravery in battle and consisted of glory among men, the praise of those still living. The poet's last word about the hero Beowulf in the poem which now bears his name is *lofgeornost* 'most eager for fame'. Two comments from the same poem throw light on this concept:

> Swa sceal man don,
> þonne he æt guðe   gegan þenceð
> longsumne lof;   na ymb his lif cearað

'So must a man do when he thinks to win enduring fame in battle; he will show no concern for his life' and

> Wyrd oft nereð
> unfægne eorl,   þonne his ellen deah!

'Fate often spares an undoomed man when his courage is good.'

A warrior brought up in this tradition would show a reckless disregard for his life. Whether he was doomed or not, courage was best, for the brave man could win *lof* while the coward might die before his time. This is the spirit which inspired the code of the *comitatus*. While his lord lived, the warrior owed him loyalty unto death. If his lord were killed, the warrior had to avenge him or die in the attempt. The lord in his turn had the duty of protecting the warriors. He had to be a great fighter to attract men, a man of noble character and a generous giver of feasts and treasures to hold them. So we read in *The Finnesburh Fragment*

> Ne gefrægn ic næfre wurþlicor   æt wera hilde
> sixtig sigebeorna   sel gebæran,
> ne nefre swanas hwitne medo   sel forgyldan
> ðonne Hnæfe guldan   his hægstealdas

'I have never heard it said that sixty conquering warriors bore themselves better or more worthily in mortal combat, or that any retainers repaid the shining mead better than Hnæf's retainers repaid him.'

The whole code receives one of its last and finest expressions in *The Battle of Maldon*, especially in the oft-quoted lines spoken by the old warrior Byrhtwold

> Hige sceal þe heardra,   heorte þe cenre,
> mod sceal þe mare,   þe ure mægen lytlað

'Courage must be the firmer, heart the bolder, spirit the greater, the more our strength wanes.' Here we see a noble manifestation of 'man's unconquerable mind'.

Sometimes a conflict arose between loyalty to *comitatus* and loyalty to kin. The annal for 755 in the Parker Manuscript of the *Chronicle* tells us of warriors who, in reply to offers of safe-conduct and money from kinsmen in a hostile force, said that 'no kinsman was dearer to them than their lord, and they would never follow his slayer'. This seems to have been the proper attitude. But, as Professor Whitelock points out, the fact that the Laws of Alfred allow a man to fight in defence of a wronged kinsman only if it did not involve fighting against his lord suggests that the claims of kin sometimes overrode the duty to a lord.

A woman given in marriage as a *freoðuwebbe* 'a peace-weaver' to patch up a blood feud was often involved in such a conflict between loyalty to her lord, her husband, on the one hand and to her family on the other. Freawaru was in this position, Hildeburh may have been; both feature in

Beowulf. Sigemund's sister Signy was also involved in such a conflict of loyalties, although in her case the feud arose after the marriage. Thus the 'eternal triangle' of Anglo-Saxon literature is based on loyalty rather than on sexual love (though such poems as *The Wife's Lament* and *The Husband's Message* show that such love existed — if we need any assuring on the point). No woman inspired the hero Beowulf, as far as we know. The great love of heroic literature is that of man for man in the noblest sense, the loyalty of warrior to warrior and of warrior to lord. This is not peculiar to the Anglo-Saxons. In the *Chanson de Roland*, Roland's betrothed Aude receives passing mention — even that is perhaps unusual — but Roland's great love is for Oliver. Just before his last battle, Roland cries to Oliver:

> For his liege lord a man ought to suffer all hardship and endure great heat and great cold and give both his body and his blood. Lay on with thy lance and I will smite with Durendal, my good sword which the King gave me. If I die here, may he to whom it shall fall say: 'This was the sword of a goodly vassal.'

Again, in his book *Island of the Dragon's Blood*, Douglas Botting tells the story of a sixteenth-century battle between Portuguese and Arabs on the island of Socotra. The Portuguese leader, Tristan da Cunha, offered the Arabs terms. The story goes on:

> But the Arabs replied that they were much obliged to the worthy chief captain for wishing to spare their lives but that, in telling them of their captain's death, he had given them a sufficient reason for declining to receive the favour, for the Fartaquins [Mahri Arabs] were not accustomed to return alive to their land and leave their captain dead on the field, especially as he was the son of their King. Therefore he might do as he pleased for they were not going to yield.

But it is important to grasp that this loyalty is fundamental to much Old English poetry. Of course, the time was not far distant when the interest of writers switched from the 'heroic' love of man for man to the 'romantic' love of man for woman. C. S. Lewis characterizes the change which then came over European literature as a revolution compared to which 'the Renaissance is a mere ripple on the surface of literature'.

Among the members of the *comitatus*, there was an insistence on decorum and etiquette — *cupe he duguðe þeaw* 'he knew the usages of noble warriors' observes the *Beowulf* poet at one point — a respect for well-tried weapons, a love of precious jewels and beautiful things, joy in ships and in warriors marching, in horse races and beer, and in feasting and music in the hall. There was too a pride in being a well-governed people. The hall was an oasis of comradeship, order, warmth, and happiness, in sharp contrast to the threatening and chaotic world of discomfort and danger which lay outside. Old English poetry is not made up entirely of gloomy moments. Sometimes there is laughter and mirth.

But there is also a great awareness of the transitoriness of life — *þis læne lif* 'this transitory life' sings the poet. The answer of the Northumbrian chief to King Edwin's question 'Shall we become Christians?' (translated here from the Old English *Bede*) gives a vivid insight into how he saw life:

O King, in comparison with that time which is unknown to us, the life we now lead on earth seems to me thus: as if you were sitting at a feast in the winter-time with your chiefs and your thanes. Inside the fire is burning and the hall is warm. Outside it is raining and snowing, and the storm rages. Then there comes a sparrow and flies quickly through the hall — in one door and out the other. While he is inside, he is unbuffeted by the storm of winter. But that is for no time at all, just the twinkling of an eye, for he passes straight from winter to winter. Similarly, a human life exists for a brief moment of time; what goes before it and what follows after it, we do not know.

Some critics of Old English literature sometimes talk as if this were an idea peculiar to Germanic or Anglo-Saxon paganism. But other peoples have grasped the idea that life is transitory. Numerous passages could be cited from Greek and

Latin authors. Rider Haggard quotes a Zulu saying that life is 'as the breath of oxen in winter, as the quick star that runs along the sky, as the little shadow that loses itself at sunset'. A famous passage in *The Wisdom of Solomon*, chapter V, compares the passing of the things of this earth to the passage of a shadow, of a ship in the waves, and of a bird or an arrow through the air. In *James*, chapter IV, we read that life is 'a vapour that appeareth for a little time, and then vanisheth away'. We should therefore view with suspicion any comment on such poems as *The Wanderer* and *The Seafarer* which draws unreal distinctions between pagan and Christian elements as a result of failure to realize that the transience of life is a perpetual human theme peculiar to no civilization, age, or culture.

This theme of transience receives frequent expression in Old English poetry. Two fine examples are the famous lines at the end of *The Wanderer* and a passage from the less-known *Solomon and Saturn*:

> Lytle hwile   leaf beoð grene;
> ðonne hie eft fealewiað,   feallað on eorðan
> and forweorniað,   weorðað to duste

'For a little while the leaves are green. Then they turn yellow, fall to the earth and perish, turning to dust.' But, while the theme is universal, the response is often different. In both *The Wanderer* and *The Dream of the Rood* the passing of friends is lamented. But whereas in *The Wanderer* the thought provokes the famous response 'Where are they now?', the dreamer who has gazed upon the Cross affirms triumphantly that they live now in Heaven with the King of Glory.

The transitoriness of all joys was brought home with special force to the man without a lord, always a figure of misery in Old English literature. He may have survived his lord because he was a coward who ran away from battle, like the sons of Odda in *The Battle of Maldon*, or by fortune of war which decreed that he was badly wounded, but not killed, like the two survivors of the fights in the already-mentioned annal for 755. He may even have betrayed his lord, like Ceolwulf, the foolish king's thane who ruled Mercia as a Danish puppet for a few years after 874. Because of this uncertainty, a lordless man was suspect wherever he went. We can perhaps to some extent conceive his misery if we ponder the state of mind of people who find themselves in one of the following situations today — a trade-unionist expelled from his union and unable to earn money by his only skill; an army-officer or an administrator suddenly expelled without compensation from a former colonial territory where he had made his career; a discharged convict unable to get a job; or a lonely refugee from behind the Iron Curtain who has left dear ones behind him and now exists without hope in a camp for 'displaced persons'.

What joy and hope the coming of Christianity in the sixth century must have brought to such a man! And not to him alone, but also to those safely within a *comitatus*. For even they had little, if any, belief in a personal after-life, and no awareness of what Professor Southern has called 'the personal and secret tie between man and God'. Surrounded by few of the material comforts we take for granted today, liable to sudden attack and without any real hope for the future, they too must have found in Christianity the peace which passeth understanding. Doubtless, it was still true that

> Forðon sceall gar wesan
> monig morgenceald   mundum bewunden,
> hæfen on handa,   nalles hearpan sweg
> wigend weccean,   ac se wonna hrefn

'For many a spear, cold with the chill of morning, must be grasped with the palms, lifted by the hand. No sound of harp shall wake the warriors, but the dark raven.' But now the warriors could lie down under the protection of the Almighty and could rise with the name of Christ upon their lips.

To be sure, conversion was neither universal nor immediate. But those who experienced it must have been a strange blend of pagan and Christian, combining as they did the fierce courage and pride of paganism with the new hope derived from Christianity — a blend strikingly seen on the Benty

Grange helmet which bears both the pagan boar and the Christian Cross. Something of the same (but in reverse) must, one imagines, be part of the make-up of those middle-aged and elderly Russians of today who were brought up Christians but who have consciously or unconsciously been influenced by the teachings of Marx. In 1961 Mr. Khrushchev was reported as saying that the Soviet Union possessed a 100-megaton bomb 'which, God grant it, we may never have to explode'. Whether this invocation of God was deliberately cynical, the accidental result of thought-habits formed in youth, or proof that he really is a Christian at heart, one cannot say. But the fact that he could call on God will help us to understand why the *Beowulf* poet could say in the same poem both

> Wyrd oft nereð
> unfægne eorl, þonne his ellen deah!

'Fate often spares an undoomed man, when his courage is good' and

> Swa mæg unfæge eaðe gedigan
> wean ond wræcsið se ðe Waldendes
> hyldo gehealdeþ!

'Thus may an undoomed man whom the grace of God protects easily survive misery and banishment.'

From this it follows that a poem which contains distinctly pagan and distinctly Christian ideas (as opposed to one which deals with themes common to both, such as the transience of life) need not be a Christian reworking of a pagan poem. Its author may have been a converted pagan, or, like thousands of middle-aged Russians today, a man who, because he had lived with survivors of a past civilization, could grasp its values imaginatively and appreciate them even while he himself belonged to a new age.

We have heard recently of Roman Catholic missionaries in Africa singing the Mass to the rhythms of a Congo war-chant, and of the weaving of native songs and dances into the same church's baptismal ceremony in New Guinea.

Missionaries in Anglo-Saxon England similarly 'baptized' pagan institutions, methods, and concepts. The Yeavering excavations give evidence of a pagan temple converted to Christian use. Bede's account of the poet Cædmon tells how, between 657 and 680, Cædmon sang his famous *Hymn* and so used heroic alliterative verse for Christian purposes — a development of great importance for Old English literature. And in *The Seafarer* we find the pagan idea of *lof* Christianized — it now consists of praise on earth and life in Heaven and is to be won by fighting against the Devil and by doing good.

If we bear all this in mind, the incongruities to which our attention is so often drawn by critics of Old English poetry will trouble us less. After all, we can today 'thank our lucky stars' and say 'By Jove!' without believing that the stars really influence our lives or that Jupiter will protect us in battle. Similarly, if we find that our own interpretation of *Beowulf* commits us to the view that its author was a passionate believer in Christianity, we need not be deterred by the fact that he speaks of the power of *wyrd*.

These problems loom large in Old English literature because we know very little about the genesis of most poems. The titles are modern, and sometimes misleading. *Cædmon's Hymn* is attributed to Cædmon, and four poems — *Fates of the Apostles*, *Elene*, *Juliana*, and *Christ II* — bear Cynewulf's 'signature' in runes. But this does not give us much help, for Cynewulf is little more than a name. The unfortunate fact is that we just do not know for whom, by whom, when, where, or with what aim, most of the poems were written. This inevitably creates difficulties for us when we try to elucidate them and may lead us to criticize a poem for not having a structure which appeals to us or for not being the poem we think it ought to be.

VI. ALLITERATIVE VERSE

Because of these difficulties we must make a special effort to understand, as far as we can, the conventions within which the Anglo-Saxon poets were writing. For, in the words of

Alan Bliss, 'Old English poetry is not at all primitive; on the contrary, it is very highly artificial and sophisticated'. The natural question 'In what ways?' can be answered by a consideration of the metrical form, the vocabulary, and the poets' handling of certain themes and their response to certain situations.

In general, Old English poetry tends to fall into verse paragraphs with enjambement between the lines and with frequent repetition. The demands of alliteration make this repetition necessary. In the hands of the feeble craftsman, of course, it is often empty. But the good poet, by varying his point and by giving additional information, is able to enrich his verse. A simple illustration on a not particularly high level may help to explain this.

In *The Battle of Maldon*, lines 113–15, we read:

> Wund wearð Wulfmær, wælræste geceas,
> Byrhtnoðes mæg, he mid billum wearð,
> his swustersunu, swiðe forheawen.

Literally glossed this means

> Wounded became Wulfmær, rest among the slain chose,
> Byrhtnoth's kinsman, he with swords became,
> his sister's son, cruelly hewn down.

Here the first half-line tells the whole story in brief. The remaining first half-lines tell us who Wulfmær was — the kinsman of the English commander and (more important) his sister's son, which, as Tacitus pointed out, was a particularly important tie in Germanic society. The second half-lines all fill out the word 'wounded' — he was fatally wounded, he was wounded by swords, he was cruelly wounded. Here we see in simple form the technique of repetition with variation and advance.

Within the verse paragraph, the alliterative unit is the line. The alliteration falls on accented syllables. The first accented syllable of the second half-line ('the head-stave') gives the alliterating letter. Thus in the quotation above, line 113 alliterates on *w* (*wund . . . Wulf . . . wæl*; the unaccented

c

wearð is not part of the scheme), line 114 on *b* (*Byrht . . . bill*), and line 115 on *sw*. The maximum number of alliterations in any one line is three (as in line 113). The minimum — naturally enough — is two, one in each half-line.

But the metrical unit is the half-line, and the metrical patterns were selected from those common in ordinary speech. In the strict 'classical verse' — preserved or resurrected in *The Battle of Brunanburh* — only certain patterns were admitted. *The Battle of Maldon* admits other patterns and is therefore in a technical sense 'careless'. But it does not degenerate into doggerel, as do some of the later poems not represented here.

A few examples will suffice to show the close relationship between verse rhythms and those of prose. One common pattern (know as type A) is 'stress unstress stress unstress'. The following are some of the combinations which often fall into that pattern:

adjective + noun (*lāðe gystas* 'hateful strangers'),
subject + verb (*beornas fēollon* 'warriors fell'),
object + verb (*gāras bǣron* 'spears [they] carried'),
complement + verb (*gearwe stōdon* 'ready stood'),
infinitive + verb (*wealdan mōston* 'to wield were able'),
and noun + adjective (*wīges georne* 'for war eager').

Again, *brimlīþendra* is the genitive plural of a present participle used as a noun 'of the seafarers'. By itself it makes up a half-line of the pattern Da described below.

There are six of these basic patterns and each half-line is an example or a variation of one of them. Professor Tolkien has given us the following Modern English examples of the normal forms of these six patterns:

A	falling — falling	*knights in armour*
B	rising — rising	*the roaring sea*
C	clashing	*on high mountains*
Da	falling by stages	*bright archangels*
Db	broken fall	*bold brazenfaced*
E	fall and rise	*highcrested elms*

He goes on to observe:

> These are the normal patterns of four elements into which
> Old English words naturally fell, and into which modern
> English words still fall. They can be found in any passage
> of prose, ancient or modern. Verse of this kind differs from
> prose, *not* in rearranging words to fit a special rhythm,
> repeated or varied in successive lines, but in choosing the
> simpler and more compact word-patterns and clearing away
> extraneous matter, so that these patterns stand opposed to
> one another.

Part of the artificiality of Old English poetry lay in the
restricted number of patterns permitted. Part lay in the special
poetic vocabulary, especially in the poetic compounds and in
the number of archaic words retained for their alliterative
value. Here should be noted the kenning, a sort of condensed
metaphor in which (*a*) is compared to (*b*) without (*a*) or the
point of the comparison being made explicit; the metaphor
'The camel is the ship of the desert' would become the kenning
'The desert ship lurched on.' Thus one Old English poet tells
us of a ship out-of-control and driven by the storm in the
words 'The sea-steed heeds not the bridle', while the *Exodus*
poet speaks of minstrels as 'laughter-smiths'. An audience
would require time to grasp the implications of such sophisti-
cated 'riddling' comparisons; this and the fact that there
seems to have been a harp accompaniment would suggest
that Old English poetry was recited much more slowly than
modern poetry.

Another important point about Old English poetry is that
the formulae inherited from the days when the poetry was
composed orally survive in the lettered poetry. These formulae
are set metrical combinations which can be varied according
to the needs of alliteration. Thus the phrase 'on the sea' can
be expressed by *on hranrāde* 'on the whale-road' or by *on
seglrāde* 'on the sail-road', and a lord may be a *frēawine* 'lord-
friend' or a *goldwine* 'gold-friend'. Similar variations exist for

many other expressions, e.g. 'deprived of joys' (a phrase frequently used of an exile), the epic formula 'we have heard, . . .' and the Christian concepts of God.

These formulae often cluster about a particular theme. Thus the exile — the man cut off from his *comitatus* — becomes a symbol of misery and the poets work the changes on phrases traditionally associated with this idea. Similarly the beasts of battle — the wolf, the raven, and the eagle — are to be found when a battle is imminent. Eager for carrion, they utter their grim howls and cries. Originally, they were doubtless a reality on the battlefield as they devoured the bodies of the slain; later their appearance is conventional and often, in the hands of the clumsy or uninspired poet, perfunctory. It is an interesting confirmation of the genius of the *Beowulf* poet that his is the most brilliant handling of this theme — not only in the detailed treatment, but also in the significant place it has in the over-all structure of the poem.

Whether a Christian poet was successful or not would depend in part, of course, on his own ability. But his choice of subject was also important. It has already been pointed out that the stories of *Exodus* and *Judith* fitted more readily into the conventions of heroic verse than the lives of the apostles and saints, on whom the Germanic warrior's armour sits uneasily. Similarly the situation of Satan, the rebellious and exiled thane who (as the poet with intentional irony shows us in the passage from *Genesis B* translated above) expected loyalty from his own followers, would find a readier response in an Anglo-Saxon warrior than would the story of King Edmund of East Anglia, who threw away his weapons when confronted by his Danish foes 'because he wished to imitate the example of Christ'. The problem was even more difficult for the poet handling questions of Christian theology in alliterative verse. The Anglo-Saxon Christian poet seems to have been in a position akin to that of the Jugoslav oral poets during the Second World War; the Marxist heroes could be made to acquire the characteristics of earlier folk-heroes perhaps without too much trouble, but Marxist dialectic —

like Christian theology in Anglo-Saxon times — proved a tougher nut.

In concluding this section, I cannot do better than quote the remarks of Alan Bliss:

> The appreciation of Old English poetry cannot be learned in a day, but it can be learned without great difficulty, provided it is approached in the right spirit. The student must remember that, although Old English poetry resembles Modern English poetry in many ways, it is nevertheless very different from it. He must not expect to find a regularly recurring rhythm such as is found in Modern English until fairly recently; rather he must learn to recognize (and admire) the way in which the natural rhythms of English speech are organized into a poetic vehicle of immense power and flexibility, capable of achieving the most subtle and varied effects. Reading aloud is very helpful; if the proper stresses, quantities and pauses are observed, the poetic qualities will soon make themselves felt. The student of today, familiar as he is with various varieties of 'free verse', is probably better equipped to appreciate Old English poetry to the full than the student of any previous generation.

In doing so, he will find that alliterative verse is capable of varied and powerful effects. Some Old English examples have already been quoted. That variety can be achieved is clear from *Beowulf*, lines 210–18, where the gentle rocking of the ship at anchor in a protected harbour, the busy bustle of the warriors as they load it, the heaviness of the ship as the oarsmen shove off, and its magical transformation into a light and living thing as it flies like a bird before the wind, are all reflected in the verse itself. The passage from *The Dream of the Rood* analysed in Appendix I shows the heights to which Old English verse could rise.

The survival of the alliterative measure until its glorious flowering in the late fourteenth century should be noted. Here too it rises to greatness; witnesses to this are the *Gawain* poet, with his lively dialogue and his splendid nature descriptions, and Langland, who achieves nobility in passages from *Piers Plowman* such as this:

'*Consummatum est*', quod Cryst · and comsed forto swowe
Pitousliche and pale · as a prisoun that deyeth;
The lorde of lyf and of liʒte · tho leyed his eyen togideres.
The daye for drede with-drowe · and derke bicam the sonne,
The wal wagged and clef · and al the worlde quaued.
Ded men for that dyne · come out of depe graues,
And tolde whi that tempest · so longe tyme dured.
'For a bitter bataille' · the ded bodye sayde;
'Lyf and Deth in this derknesse · her one fordoth her other;
Shal no wiʒte wite witterly · who shal haue the maystrye,
Er Sondey aboute sonne-rysynge' · and sank with that til erthe.
Some seyde that he was goddes sone · that so faire deyde,
             Vere filius dei erat iste, etc.
And somme saide he was a wicche · 'good is that we assaye,
Where he be ded or nouʒte ded · doun er he be taken'.

THE BATTLE OF MALDON

The Battle of Maldon is an appropriate beginning for our book. It is the first Old English poem read by most students of the language and is one of the best battle poems in English. The original manuscript was lost in the Cottonian fire of 1731, but the poem survives in an edition printed in the eighteenth century and in the earlier transcript on which this was based. A little has been lost at the beginning and the end. While generally following tradition in vocabulary and style, the poem shows some metrical irregularities not permitted in 'classical' Old English and makes occasional use of rhyme. But it is worthy of its theme; it deals very successfully with a contemporary event and, like the warriors whose praises it sings, is plain, vigorous, strong, and 'heroic'.

The battle celebrated in the poem took place in August 991, a few miles below Maldon, Essex, on the southern bank of the River Blackwater. The Danes were encamped on Northey Island, and the causeway they were allowed to cross can still be seen and is still submerged at high tide. Historically, the battle was only one of a series of minor engagements between the invading Northmen and the English; it is noteworthy (like Chalgrove Field) for the death of a distinguished leader and (more important) for what the poet has made of it.

First, he has given us a clear idea of the stages of the battle, even though he does follow the epic convention by which it is described as a series of single combats. We see the disposition of the English forces, the fight at the causeway, the Danes crossing the river with Byrhtnoth's permission. Then the battle begins and rages. With the death of Byrhtnoth and the flight of the sons of Odda and their cowardly companions comes the turning-point, and the rest of the poem is concerned with the grim resistance of the loyal warriors in the face of inevitable defeat. Typical of them is Offa, who fights and dies, and whose comments about boasters who will fail when put to the test (presented with such brilliant realism that we almost see him muttering in the hall) come so sadly true. One question emerges: Was Byrhtnoth justified in allowing the Danes to cross? The poet seems to think not, for he attributes to Byrhtnoth the quality of

28

ofermod, 'too much pride', a characteristic he shares with Satan. The accusation is perhaps at base one of irresponsibility. Platoon-commanders can take risks and win Victoria Crosses; such things are not a general's business. Yet, if Byrhtnoth had not allowed the Danes to cross, they might have sailed away and ravaged another part of Essex; hence, it could be argued, Byrhtnoth fulfilled his duty 'to seek out and destroy the enemy, wherever he may be found. . . .'

Second, the poet shows the heroic code of the *comitatus* at its best. Byrhtnoth answers the Viking messenger with grim irony; not for him the spineless attitude condemned by a later chronicler of Ethelred's reign:

> All these disasters came upon us because we had no policy in that we were neither willing to pay tribute in time nor to fight our foes. On the contrary, we made peace with them when they had done the greatest possible amount of harm. And then, despite all this truce-making and tribute-paying, they journeyed everywhere in bands, harrying, plundering, and slaying the wretched inhabitants of our land.

The warriors, including (as was proper) the Northumbrian hostage, fulfil their boast, repay the mead their lord had given them, find pleasure in battle (despite their Christianity), avenge their dead lord, and themselves lie dead beside his body. Byrhtwold's short cry epitomizes the code by which they lived and died. Love of their land and loyalty to their king (a feeling of patriotism?) reinforce their sense of duty to their lord. But the latter is still paramount; their epitaph is not *Dulce et decorum est pro patria mori*, but *he læg ðegenlice ðeodne gehende*, 'he lay, as befits a thane, close by his lord'.

THE BATTLE OF MALDON

> . . . it was shattered.
> Then *Byrhtnoth* ordered every warrior to dismount,
> Let loose his horse and go forward into battle
> With faith in his own skills and bravery.
> Thus *Offa's* young son could see for himself
> That the earl was no man to suffer slackness.
> He sent his best falcon flying from his wrist
> To the safety of the forest and strode into the fight;

The boy's behaviour was a testament
That he would not be weak in the turmoil of battle.
Eadric too was firmly resolved to follow his leader
Into the fight. At once he hurried forward
With his spear. He feared no foe
For as long as he could lift his shield
And wield a sword: he kept his word
That he would pierce and parry before his prince.

Then *Byrhtnoth* began to martial his men.
He rode about, issuing instructions
As to how they should stand firm, not yielding an inch,
And how they should tightly grip their shields
Forgetting their qualms and pangs of fear.
And when he had arrayed the warriors' ranks
He dismounted with his escort at a carefully chosen place
Where his finest troops stood prepared for the fight.
Then a spokesman for the Vikings stood on the river
        bank
And aggressively shouted
A message from the seafarers
To *Byrhtnoth*, the earl, on the opposite bank.
'The brave seafarers have sent me to say to you
That they will be so good as to let you give gold rings
In return for peace. It is better for you
To buy off our raid with gold
Than that we, renowned for cruelty, should cut you down in
        battle.
Why destroy one another? If you're good for a certain
        sum,
We'll settle for peace in exchange for gold.
If you, most powerful over there, agree to this
And wisely decide to disband your men,
Giving gold to the seafarers on their own terms
In return for a truce,
We'll take to the sea with the tribute you pay
And keep our promise of peace.'

Then *Byrhtnoth* spoke. He grasped his shield
And brandished his slender ashen spear,
Resentful and resolute he shouted his reply:
'Can you hear, you pirate, what these people say?
They will pay you a tribute of whistling spears,
Of deadly darts and proven swords,
Weapons to pay you, pierce, slit and slay you in storming
     battle.
Listen, messenger! Take back this reply:
Tell your people the unpleasant tidings
That over here there stands a noble earl with his troop —
Guardians of the people and of the country,
The home of *Ethelred*, my prince — who'll defend this
     land
To the last ditch. We'll sever the heathens' heads
From their shoulders. It would be much to our shame
If you took our tribute and embarked without battle
Since you've intruded so far
And so rudely into this country.
No! You'll not get your treasure so easily.
The spear's point and the sword's edge, savage battle-play,
Must teach us first that we have to yield tribute.'
Then *Byrhtnoth* gave word that all his warriors should walk
With their shields to the river bank.
The troops on either side could not get at one another,
For there the flood flowed after the turn of the tide;
The water streams ran together. Waiting seemed like passing
     years,
Waiting to cross and clash their spears.
The East-Saxons and the Ship-army
Stood beside the River Panta in proud array.
But no warrior could work harm on another
Except by the flight of a feathered arrow.
The tide ebbed; the pirates stood prepared,
Many bold Vikings ready for battle.
Then *Byrhtnoth*, brave protector of his men, ordered
A warrior, *Wulfstan* by name, to defend the ford.

He was *Ceola's* son, outstanding for his courage amongst
   courageous men.
He struck the first seafarer with his spear
Who fearlessly stepped onto the ford.
Two experienced warriors stood with *Wulfstan*,
Ælfere and *Maccus*, both brave men.
Nothing could have made them take flight at the ford.
They would have defended it
For as long as they could wield their weapons.
But as it was, the Danes found the dauntless guardians
Of the ford too fierce for their liking. . . .
The hateful strangers began to use guile
And asked if they could cross,
Leading their warriors over the water.
Then, in foolhardy pride, the earl permitted
Those hateful strangers to have access to the ford.
The son of *Byrhthelm* began to call out
Across the cold water (the warriors listened):
'Now the way is clear for you. Come over to us quickly,
Come to the slaughter. God alone can say
Who of us that fight today will live to fight again.'

Then the wolvish Vikings, avid for slaughter,
Waded to the west across the River Panta;
The seafarers hoisted their shields on high
And carried them over the gleaming water.
Byrhtnoth and his warriors awaited them,
Ready for battle: he ordered his men
To form a phalanx with their shields, and to stand firm
Against the onslaught of the enemy. Then was the battle,
With its chance of glory, about to begin. The time had come
For all the doomed men to fall in the fight.
The clamour began; the ravens wheeled and the eagle
Circled overhead, craving for carrion; there was shouting on
   earth.
They hurled their spears, hard as files,
And sent sharp darts flying from their hands.

Bow strings were busy, shield parried point,
Bitter was the battle. Brave men fell
On both sides, youths choking in the dust.
Byrhtnoth's sister's son, *Wulfmær*, was wounded;
Slashed by the sword, he decided
To sleep on the bed of death.
This was violently requited, the Vikings were repaid in kind.
I was told that *Eadweard* swung his sword
So savagely — a full-blooded blow —
That a fated warrior fell lifeless at his feet.
Byrhtnoth shouted out his thanks to him,
His chamberlain, as soon as he had a chance to do so.
The brave men stood resolute, rock firm.
Each of them eagerly hunted for a way
To be first in with his spear,
Winning with his weapons the life
Of a doomed warrior; the dead sank down to the earth.
But the rest stood unshaken and *Byrhtnoth* spurred them on,
Inciting each man to fight ferociously
Who wished to gain glory against the Danes.
Then a brave seafarer raised up his spear,
Gripped his shield and advanced towards *Byrhtnoth*.
The resolute earl advanced towards the churl;
Each had evil designs on the other.
The Viking was the quicker — he hurled his foreign spear
Wounding the lord of the warriors.
Byrhtnoth broke the shaft with the edge of his shield;
The imbedded spear-head sprang out of his wound.
Then he flung his spear in fury
At the proud Viking who dared inflict such pain.
His aim was skilful. The spear
Slit open the warrior's neck.
Thus *Byrhtnoth* put paid to his enemy's life.
Then, for safety's sake, he swiftly hurled another
Which burst the Viking's breastplate, cruelly wounding him
In the chest; the deadly spear pierced his heart.
The brave earl, *Byrhtnoth*, was delighted at this;

He laughed out loud and gave thanks to the Lord
That such good fortune had been granted to him.
But one of the seafarers sent a sharp javelin
Speeding from his hand
That pierced *Byrhtnoth's* body, the noble thane of *Ethelred.*
By his side stood a young warrior,
Wulfmær by name, *Wulfstan's* son,
Who without a moment's hesitation
Drew out the blood-red javelin from *Byrhtnoth's* side
And hurled it back as hard as he could
At the man who had grievously injured his prince.
The sharp point struck home; the Viking sagged, and sank into
    the dust.
Another seafarer advanced on the earl, meaning to make
Short work of him and snatch away his treasures —
His armour and his rings and his ornamented sword.

Byrhtnoth drew out his sword from its sheath,
Broad-faced and gleaming, and made to slash at the seafarer's
    corselet,
But his enemy stopped him all too soon,
Savagely striking *Byrhtnoth's* arm.
The golden-hilted sword dropped from his hand.
He could hold it no longer
Nor wield a weapon of any kind. Then the old warrior
Raised his men's morale with bold words,
Called on his brave companions to do battle again.
He no longer stood firmly on his feet
But swayed, and raised his eyes to heaven:
'O Guardian of the people, let me praise and thank you
For all the real joys I received in this world.
Now, gracious Lord, as never before,
I need Your grace,
That my soul may set out on its journey to You,
O Prince of Angels, that my soul may depart
Into Your power in peace. I pray
That the devils may never destroy it.'

Then the heathens hewed him down
And the two men who stood there supporting him;
Ælfnoth and *Wulfmær* fell to the dust,
Both gave their lives in defence of their lord.
Then certain cowards beat a hasty retreat:
The sons of *Odda* were the first to take flight;
Godric fled from the battle, forsaking *Byrhtnoth*.
Forgetting that his lord had given him often the gift of a horse,
He leapt into the saddle
Of his lord's own horse, most unlawfully,
And both his brothers, *Godwine* and *Godwig*,
Galloped beside him; forgetting their duty
They fled from the fight
And saved their lives in the silent wood.
And more men followed than was at all fitting
Had they remembered the former rewards
That the prince had given them, generous presents.
It was just as *Offa* once said to *Byrhtnoth*
At an open council in the meeting place,
That many spoke proudly of their prowess
Who would prove unworthy of their words under battle-stress.

So *Ethelred's* earl, the prince of those people,
Fell; all his hearth-companions
Could see for themselves that their lord lay low.
Then the proud thanes, with the utmost bravery,
Threw themselves once more into the thick of the battle.
They all, without exception, strove to one of two ends —
To avenge their lord or to leave this world.
Ælfwine the son of *Ælfric*, still a young man,
Shouted encouragement, urging them on.
He rallied them with valiant words:
'Think of all the times we boasted
At the mead-bench, heroes in the hall
Predicting our own bravery in battle.
Now we shall see who meant what he said.
Let me announce my ancestry to one and all:

I come from a mighty family of Mercian stock;
My grandfather was *Ealhelm*,
A wise *ealdorman*, well endowed with worldly riches.
No thane shall ever have reason to reproach me
With any desire to desert this troop
And hurry home, now that my prince has been hewn down
In battle. This is the most bitter sorrow of all.
He was my kinsman and my lord.'
Then he went forward into the fight
And pierced a pirate's body with his spear.
The man keeled over, dead,
Killed by *Ælfwine's* weapon. Again he urged
His friends and companions
To follow him into the fray.
Then *Offa* spoke and brandished his ash-spear:
'*Ælfwine*, you've encouraged all the thanes
At exactly the right time. Now that our prince
Is slain, the earl on the earth,
We must all encourage each other
To fight, for as long as we can wield
Our weapons, pierce with our spears,
And lunge and parry with our swords.
Godric, the cowardly son of *Odda*, has betrayed us all.
When he hurried off toward the woods on our lord's fine horse
He misled many men into believing it was *Byrhtnoth* himself;
And so they followed him, and here on the field
The phalanx was broken: may fortune frown on him
Whose cowardice has caused this catastrophe.'
Then *Leofsunu* spoke. He raised his shield
For protection, and replied to *Offa*:
'I give you my word that I will not retreat
One inch; I shall forge on
And avenge my lord in battle.
Now that he has fallen in the fight
No loyal warrior living at Sturmere
Need reproach me for returning home lordless
In unworthy retreat, for the weapon shall take me,

The iron sword.' He strode forward angrily,
Fighting furiously; he spurned escape.
Then *Dunnere* spoke and shook his spear;
A lowly churl, he cried out loud
And asked every man to avenge *Byrhtnoth's* death:
'Whoever intends to avenge our prince
Must not flinch, nor care for his own life.'
Then they hurried forward, heedless of their lives;
The brave followers, fiercely carrying spears,
Fought with great courage, and prayed to God
That they should be allowed to avenge their lord
By killing all his enemies.
The hostage helped them with all his might —
His name was *Æscferth*, the son of *Ecglaf*;
He came from a family renowned in Northumbria.
In the fire of battle he did not flinch,
Notching arrow after arrow as quick as he could.
Sometimes he hit a shield, sometimes he pierced a man,
Again and again he inflicted wounds
For as long as he could hold a bow in his hands.

Eadweard the tall, eager and impetuous,
Did not stray from the line of battle. He boasted that he
Would not shrink so much as a footstep,
Or seek safety by flight, now that his lord lay dead.
He smashed the wall of shields, and attacked the seafarers
Worthily avenging his ring-giver's death.
He sold his life dearly in the storm of battle.
And so too did *Ætheric*, a stalwart companion. . . .
He grappled aggressively and without delay.
The brother of *Sibyrht*, both he and many others
Split the hollow shields and warded off the seafarers.
The corner of the shield broke and the corselet sang
A terrible song. Then in the turmoil
Offa struck a seafarer; he fell dead at his feet.
But the kinsman of *Gadd* was killed there too,
Offa was quickly brought down in the battle.

D

Yet he had kept his promise to his prince;
He fulfilled his former boast to *Byrhtnoth*, the ring-giver,
That they should either return unhurt, riding to the stronghold
In victory together, or together surrender their lives,
Bleeding from wounds on the battlefield.
He lay near his lord as befits a thane.
Then shields were shattered; the seafarers surged forward,
Embittered by bloodshed. Often a spear
Sank into the body of a fated warrior. Then *Wistan* advanced,
The son of *Thurstan*; he fought with the Vikings,
Slew three in the struggling throng
Before he, *Wigelm's* brave son, was himself brought down.
That was a savage fight; the warriors stood firm
In the struggle. Strong men fell,
Utterly worn out by wounds; the dead dropped to the earth.
The brothers *Oswold* and *Eadweard*
Continuously encouraged the companions;
They urged their kinsmen to use
Their weapons without slackening
And endure the stress to the best of their strength.
Byrhtwold grasped his shield and spoke.
He was an old companion. He brandished his ash-spear
And with wonderful courage exhorted the warriors:
'Mind must be the firmer, heart the more fierce,
Courage the greater, as our strength diminishes.
Here lies our leader, dead,
An heroic man in the dust.
He who now longs to escape will lament for ever.
I am old. I will not go from here,
But I mean to lie by the side of my lord,
Lie in the dust with the man I loved so dearly.'
Godric, too, the son of *Æthelgar*, gave them courage
To continue the fight. Often he let fly his spear,
His deadly javelin, at the Vikings
As he advanced at the head of the host.
He humbled and hewed down until at last he fell himself. . . .

THE BATTLE OF BRUNANBURH

The Battle of Brunanburh, the earliest and best of the poems in the *Anglo-Saxon Chronicle*, is — like the others — commemorative. It celebrates the victory of King Æthelstan of Wessex and his brother Edmund at Brunanburh in 937. These two — sons of Edward the Elder and grandsons of King Alfred — led a force of West Saxons and Mercians against an invading army of Norsemen, Britons, and Scots, who were attempting to win back control of Northumberland from King Æthelstan. The enemy leaders were Anlaf (Olaf) the Norse King of Dublin, Constantine King of the Picts and Scots, and Owen King of the Strathclyde Welsh. The exact site of the battle has not been determined. Somewhere near the sea or a large river in the north of England (perhaps, it has been suggested by Professor Dobbie, on the west coast between Chester and Dumfries) is all that can usefully be said here.

Metrically, the poem is conservative, representing (in Professor Campbell's words) 'an artificial preservation, or rather, perhaps, resurrection of the old style' which is 'equally distant from the doggerel of the popular poems of the *Chronicle*, and the vigorous, but often careless, verse of *The Battle of Maldon*'. The same conservatism is apparent in the vocabulary and imagery.

The heroic spirit shines through this poem as it does through *The Battle of Maldon*. The two royal leaders win everlasting glory as they exult in the hard handplay against their foes, while the doomed warriors fall in battle, leaving their bodies to be eaten by the wolf, the raven, and the eagle. Perhaps conventional here, this was originally a grim reality; a Celtic poet speaks of 'the eagle greedy for the flesh of one I love . . . on his white breast a black raven'. Although the brothers protect their land, treasures, and homes, it would be a mistake to detect a sense of patriotism here, for England is not yet united.

But, while *Maldon* sings of defeat, *Brunanburh* celebrates a victory in panegyric terms. While in *Maldon* we see the decisive incidents in detail, *Brunanburh* tells us little of the course of the battle. The tone of *Maldon* is one of grim defiance; that of *Brunanburh* is one of scorn, exultation, and grim triumph. This emerges, not only in the typical understatements that the foe had no reason to exult, to boast, or to laugh, or in the gloating accounts of the death or flight of kings, but also in the boastful claim that it was the greatest of all English victories — a sentence which smacks of the extravagant claims of modern advertising and confirms the impression that the poem is the work of an Anglo-Saxon publicity man, whose aim was to glorify the royal family of Wessex. But in so doing, he made a poem.

THE BATTLE OF BRUNANBURH

Æthelstan the King, ruler of earls
And ring-giver to men, and Prince *Eadmund*
His brother, earned this year fame everlasting
With the blades of their swords in battle
At Brunanburh; with their well-wrought weapons
Both *Eadweard's* sons cleaved the linden shields,
Cut through the phalanx; as was only fitting
For men of their descent, they often carried arms
Against some foe in defence of their land,
Their treasure, their homes. The enemy perished,
Doomed Scots and seafarers
Fell in the fight; from the hour when that great
Constellation the sun, the burning candle
Of God eternal, first glides above the earth
Until at last that lordly creation
Sinks into its bower, the battlefield flowed
With dark blood. Many a warrior lay there,
Spreadeagled by spears, many a Norse seafarer
Stabbed above his shield and many a weary Scot,
Surfeited by war. All day,
In troops together, the West Saxons
Pursued those hateful people,
Hewed down the fugitives fiercely from behind
With their sharpened swords. The Mercians did not stint
Hard handplay to any of the heroes
Who, fated to fight, sought this land

With *Anlaf*, sailed in the ship's hold
Over the surging sea. Five young kings
Sprawled on that field of battle,
Put to sleep by swords; likewise seven
Of *Anlaf's* earls and countless in the host,
Seafarers and Scots. There, the Norse king
Was forced to flee, driven to the ship's prow
With a small bodyguard; the little ship
Scurried out to sea, the king sped
Over the dark waves and so saved his life.
Constantine, too, (a man of discretion)
Fled north to the comforts of his own country;
Deprived of kinsmen and comrades cut down
In the strife, that old warrior
Had no reason whatsoever to relish
The swordplay; he left his son
Savaged by weapons on that field of slaughter,
A mere boy in battle. That wily, grizzled warrior
Had no grounds at all to boast about
The fight, and neither did *Anlaf*;
Their army lacerated, they could scarcely exult
That things went their own way
In the thick of battle — at the clash of standards
And the encounter of spears, at the conflict of weapons
And struggle of men — when they grappled
On that field of slaughter with *Eadweard's* sons.
Then the Norsemen made off in their nailed boats,
Saddened survivors shamed in battle,
They crossed the deep water from Dingesmere
To the shelter of Dublin, Ireland once more.
Likewise both brothers together,
King and prince, returned to Wessex,
Their own country, exulting in war.
They left behind them to devour the corpses,
Relish the carrion, the horny-beaked raven
Garbed in black, and the grey-coated
Eagle (a greedy war-hawk)

With its white tail, and that grey beast,
The wolf in the wood. Never, before this,
Were more men in this island
Slain by the sword's edge —
As books and aged sages
Will confirm — since the far-off days
When Angles and Saxons sailed here from the east,
Sought the Britons over the wide seas,
Since those warsmiths hammered the Welsh,
And ambitious earls overran the land.

THE FINNESBURH FRAGMENT

The Finnesburh Fragment, like the Old High German *Hildebrandslied*, is all that survives of a Germanic 'lay' intended for recitation to the listening warriors in the hall. Professor Campbell tells us that 'lay employs a brief technique of narrative, with compressed description and rapid conversation, while epic expands in all three fields'. These characteristics can be seen in this Fragment if it is compared with any epic.

The story of the fight in Finnesburh in which Hnæf and his followers were attacked in a hall by their foes has been told in allusive fashion in *Beowulf*. It has given rise to much controversy. It is not clear exactly who began the fight, why they did, or when it took place. There is disagreement about how long the fight lasted. There are numerous other difficulties. But this much can be said in elucidation of the Fragment. Finn, King of the Frisians, has married the Danish princess Hildeburh, perhaps to patch up an existing feud between the two peoples. They have a son. While Hildeburh's brother Hnæf is visiting them at Finnesburh, he and his followers are surprised and treacherously attacked in their hall by Finn's retainers, possibly without his knowledge. At the end of the fight, Hnæf and his sister's son are both dead. It is generally (though not universally) agreed that the lay of which this Fragment forms part told of this battle. The *Beowulf* poet takes the story further and handles it with a different aim and emphasis; he uses the story to illuminate his poem and is concerned with the pathetic situation of Hildeburh, who has lost both son and brother, and with the tragic dilemmas of the other protagonists — Finn and the new Danish leader Hengest (identified by some with the Hengest who, according to the *Chronicle*, came to Britain with Horsa in 449). With him, the emphasis is on the 'pity (rather than the glory) of it all'.

But in the Fragment we feel the joy of battle. Here we have a situation which is brilliantly portrayed in another connexion by the *Beowulf* poet — the dawn attack when the warriors in the hall, awakened, not by the sound of the harp to face a new day of happiness with their comrades, but by the foreboding cry of the dark raven, must start from their sleep to grasp the spear cold with the

chill of morning. But the chill of the spear does not find its way to
the hearts of Hnæf's followers. True to their code, they rush to the
doors to fight against odds in defence of a narrow place — a typi-
cally heroic situation; compare the Spartans at Thermopylae,
Horatius and his companions at the bridge, and Wulfstan and his at
the causeway in *The Battle of Maldon*. Thus they repay the shining
mead as well as men can; 'they held the doors. . . .'

THE FINNESBURH FRAGMENT

'. . . the gables are not burning.'
Then the young king spoke, a novice in battle:
'This light is not the light of dawn; no fiery dragon flies over-
    head;
The gables of this hall are not lit up with licking flames;
But men draw near with shining weapons. The birds of battle
    screech,
The grey wolf howls, the spear rattles,
Shield answers shaft. The pale moon wanders
On her way below the clouds, gleaming; evil deeds will now
    be done
Provoking pitched battle.
Wake up now, my warriors!
Grasp your shields, steel yourselves,
Step forward and be brave!'
So many a thane, ornamented in gold, buckled his sword-belt.
Then the stout warriors, *Sigeferth* and *Eaha*
Strode to one door and unsheathed their swords;
Ordlaf and *Guthlaf* went to guard the other,
And *Hengest* himself followed in their footsteps.
When he saw this, *Guthere* said to *Garulf*
That he would be unwise to go to the hall doors
In the first fury of the onslaught, risking his precious life,
For *Sigeferth* the strong was set upon his death.
But *Garulf*, a hero of great heart,
Shouted out, 'Who holds the door?'

'I am *Sigeferth*, a warrior of the Secgan
And a well-known campaigner; I've lived through many
    conflicts,
Many stern trials. Here, in strife with me,
You'll discover your fate, victory or defeat.'
Then the din of battle broke out in the hall;
The hollow shield, defender of the body, was doomed to
    disintegrate
In the hero's hand; the hall floor boomed.
Then *Garulf*, the son of *Guthlaf*, gave his life
In the fight, first of all the warriors
Living in that land, and many heroes lay prostrate beside him.
A crowd of pale faces fell to the earth. The raven wheeled,
Dusky, dark brown. The gleaming swords so shone
It seemed as if all Finnesburh were in flames.
I have never heard, before or since, of sixty triumphant
    warriors
Who bore themselves more bravely in the thick of battle.
And never did retainers repay their prince more handsomely
For his gift of glowing mead than did those men repay *Hnæf*.
They fought five days and not one of the followers
Fell, but they held the doors firmly.
Then *Guthere* retired, worn out and wounded;
He said that his armour was almost useless,
His corselet broken, his helmet burst open.
The guardian of those people asked him at once
How well the warriors had survived their wounds
Or which of the young men. . . .

THE RIDDLES

THERE are three groups of riddles in the Exeter Book, containing ninety-six riddles in all; one of them is in Latin. They vary greatly in length and the text of some is very incomplete because of a long diagonal burn in the manuscript. In fact the Exeter Book has had some pretty rough treatment in its time — it has apparently been used as a cutting-board and in another place a beer-mug (or 'something similar') has made brown stains on several pages.

It has been claimed that the *Riddles* are the work of one author. This has not been proved and the balance of probabilities is against it. Their sources vary. Some are based on Latin riddles; some make use of traditional materials; some are perhaps original in theme and certainly original in treatment.

As their 'kennings' (condensed metaphors) suggest, riddling seems to have appealed to the Anglo-Saxons. A recent reviewer somewhat patronizingly remarked of some of these riddles that 'they are not very mysterious. No doubt thane and ealdorman knitted shaggy brows over them when they were new-minted . . . .' No doubt. But there are no titles in the manuscript and in some cases at any rate the brow-knitting operations of editors have saved us some brow-knitting of our own. In others, as Professor Kennedy has remarked, 'the riddler has yielded the pen to the descriptive poet'.

Those translated here are a cross-section of the ninety-six. They reflect many aspects of our ancestors' lives — the everyday and menial side not seen in heroic poetry; the scribe and his manuscripts; life in the hall; weapons and armour; natural life — birds, animals, and fish; ships and the sea; other phenomena of nature — ice, fire, storms, sun and moon; and the realization that God exists. They are arranged here in an order which conforms roughly to these subject-divisions.

They vary in literary merit. Some are trite, barren exercises, some show freshness and vigour. There are the ingenious and grotesque, the amusing, the satirical, and the crudely realistic and physical (these last are not represented here). Some show a knowledge of folk-lore and superstition, while others are fine pieces of natural

description based on close observation. The best show an awareness
of the magic and mystery of life and of the power of God, and trans-
mit this feeling to us.

A ONE-EYED SELLER OF ONIONS

A creature came shuffling where there sat
Many wise men in the meeting-place.
He had two ears and only one eye,
He had two feet and twelve hundred heads,
A back, two hands, and a belly,
Two shoulders and sides, a neck,
And two arms. Now tell me his name.

RAKE

A strange object caught my eye, used to feed cattle
By men of every town; it has many teeth
And is useful to men as it scrapes around, its face
To the ground. It plunders greedily, searching for plants
Along the grassy slopes, and brings them home;
It always finds those which are not rooted firmly,
But leaves the beautiful living flowers behind,
Quietly standing where they spring from the soil,
Brightly gleaming, blooming, growing.

BELLOWS

I saw a creature: his stomach stuck out behind him,
Enormously swollen. A stalwart servant
Waited upon him. What filled up his stomach
Had travelled from far, and flew through his eye.
He does not always die in giving life
To others, but new strength revives
In the pit of his stomach; he breathes again.
He fathers a son; he's his own father also.

BOOKWORM

A moth devoured words. When I heard of that wonder
It struck me as a strange event
That a worm should swallow the song of some man,
A thief gorge in the darkness on a great man's
Speech of distinction. The thievish stranger
Was not a whit the wiser for swallowing words.

PEN AND FINGERS

I watched four fair creatures
Travelling together; they left black tracks
Behind them. The support of the bird
Moved swiftly; it flew in the sky,
Dived under the waves. The struggling warrior
Continuously toiled, pointing out the paths
To all four over the fine gold.

Note: The *four creatures* are the thumb, two fingers and the pen, a quill
which as a feather had once supported the swift bird and is now dipped in
ink. The *struggling warrior* is the arm, and the *gold* is the illuminated manu-
script.

BIBLE-CODEX

An enemy ended my life, deprived me
Of my physical strength; then he dipped me
In water and drew me out again,
And put me in the sun where I soon shed
All my hair. After that, the knife's sharp edge
Bit into me and all my blemishes were scraped away;
Fingers folded me and the bird's feather
Often moved over my brown surface,
Sprinkling meaningful marks; it swallowed more wood-dye

(Part of the stream) and again travelled over me
Leaving black tracks. Then a man bound me,
He stretched skin over me and adorned me
With gold; thus I am enriched by the wondrous work
Of smiths, wound about with shining metal.
Now my clasp and my red dye
And these glorious adornments bring fame far and wide
To the Protector of Men, and not to the pains of hell.
If only the sons of men would make use of me
They would be the safer and the more victorious,
Their hearts would be bolder and their minds more at ease,
Their thoughts would be more wise; and they would have
    more friends,
Companions and kinsmen, (courageous, honourable,
Trusty, kind) who would gladly increase
Their honour and prosperity, and heap
Benefits upon them, ever holding them
Most dear. Ask what I am called,
Of such use to men. My name is famous,
Of service to men and sacred in itself.

WEATHERCOCK

My breast is puffed up and my neck is swollen.
I've a fine head and a high waving tail,
Ears and eyes also but only one foot;
A long neck, a strong beak, a back and
Two sides, and a rod right through my middle.
My home is high above men. When he who moves
The forest molests me, I suffer a great deal of misery.
Scourged by the rainlash, I stand alone;
I'm bruised by heavy batteries of hail,
Hoar frost attacks and snow half-hides me.
I must endure all this, not pour out my misery.

E

MEAD

Favoured by men, I am found far and wide,
Taken from woods and the heights of the town,
From high and from low. During each day
Bees' wings brought me through the bright sky
Skilfully home to a safe shelter. Soon after that
I was taken by men and bathed in a tub.
Now I bind and I chasten them, and cast
A young man at once to the ground, and sometimes an old
   one too.
He who struggles against my strength,
He who dares grapple with me, discovers immediately
That he will hit the hard floor with his back
If he persists with such stupidity.
Deprived of his strength, and strangely loquacious,
He's a nincompoop, who rules neither his mind
Nor his hands nor his feet. Now ask me, my friends,
Who knocks young men stupid, and as his slaves binds them
In broad, waking daylight? Yes, ask me my name.

HORN

I'm loved by my lord, and his shoulder
Companion, I'm the comrade of a warrior,
A friend of the King. Frequently the fair-haired
Queen, the daughter of an earl, deigns
To lay her hand upon me in spite of her nobility.
I carry within me what grew in the grove.
Sometimes I ride on a proud steed
At the head of the host; harsh is my voice.
Very often I recompense the gleeman
For his songs. I'm sombre in colour,
And kind at heart. What am I called?

Note: The horn is sometimes slung across the shoulder. At other times it is
filled with mead, which *grew in the grove*. It is handed to men in the hall by
the Queen or by the lord's wife, an Anglo-Saxon custom. It was also given to
the gleeman as a reward for his songs. Its harsh note sounds in battle.

BATTERING RAM

I saw a tree towering in the wood
In vestments of bright green; the timber grew,
A joyous growth. Both water and earth
Provided for it generously, but when it grew old
In times long ago, it was treated most terribly;
Sorely wounded, and sullen in its chains,
Its front was fettered with sombre trappings.
And now with brute force its butting-head
Devastates, paving the direct way
For a malicious enemy. In the mighty storm of battle
They often plunder the treasure hoard together.
Its butt is swift and restless whenever its head
Runs the gauntlet of danger for a comrade in distress.

SHIELD

I'm by nature solitary, scarred by spear
And wounded by sword, weary of battle.
I frequently see the face of war, and fight
Hateful enemies; yet I hold no hope
Of help being brought to me in the battle,
Before I'm eventually done to death.
In the stronghold of the city the sharp-edged swords,
Skilfully forged in the flame by smiths,
Bite deeply into me. I can but await
A more fearsome encounter; it is not for me
To discover in the city any of those doctors
Who heal grievous wounds with roots and herbs.
The scars from sword wounds gape wider and wider;
Death blows are dealt me by day and by night.

CUCKOO

In former days my mother and father
Forsook me for dead, for the fullness of life
Was not yet within me. But another woman
Graciously fitted me out in soft garments,
As kind to me as to her own children,
Tended and took me under her wing;
Until under her shelter, unlike her kin,
I matured as a mighty bird (as was my fate).
My guardian then fed me until I could fly,
And could wander more widely on my
Excursions; she had the less of her own
Sons and daughters by what she did thus.

SWALLOWS

This wind wafts little creatures
High over the hill-slopes. They are very
Swarthy, clad in coats of black.
They travel here and there in hordes all together,
Singing loudly, liberal with their songs.
Their haunts are wooded cliffs, yet they sometimes
Come to the houses of men. Name them yourselves.

SWAN

Silent is my dress when I step across the earth,
Reside in my house, or ruffle the waters.
Sometimes my adornments and this high windy air
Lift me over the livings of men,
The power of the clouds carries me far
Over all people. My white pinions

Resound very loudly, ring with a melody,
Sing out clearly, when I sleep not on
The soil or settle on grey waters . . . a travelling spirit.

BADGER

Whereas my neck is white, my head
And sides are brown; I'm swift of movement
And bear a battle-weapon; hair covers my back
And my cheeks as well; two ears tower high
Above my eyes. I step on my toes through
The green grass. Grief is ordained for me
If any fierce creature should catch me
In my hole where I have my house and children,
And if we linger any longer there
When this uninvited guest, the harbinger
Of death, comes knocking at the door.
Therefore I must courageously carry my infants
Far from our house, and save them by flight,
If that creature persists in pursuing me.
He advances on his breast. I dare not await him
In my hole . . . that were not a wise plan at all.
I must burrow a hole through the steep hillside
With my two forefeet as fast as I can.
I can save the lives of my loved ones
With ease, once I've guided them out
By a secret way through a hole in the hill.
Thereafter, if it comes to blows and battle
I feel no fear of this murderous foe.
If he perniciously persists in following me
Through that narrow hole I've just made in the hill,
I will not fail to offer him battle.
Once I've tunnelled my way to the top of the hill,
I will angrily batter my opponent,
That hateful foe from whom I long fled.

OYSTER

The deep sea suckled me, the waves sounded over me;
Rollers were my coverlet as I rested on my bed.
I have no feet and frequently open my mouth
To the flood. Sooner or later some man will
Consume me, who cares nothing for my shell.
With the point of his knife he will pierce me through,
Ripping the skin away from my side, and straight away
Eat me uncooked as I am. . . .

FISH AND RIVER

My abode's by no means silent, but I am not loud-mouthed.
The Lord Almighty laid down laws
For both of us together. . . . I am swifter than he who
    harbours me
And sometimes stronger too, he must strive more laboriously.
At times I quietly rest, while he must run onward.
But I live in him all the days of my life;
If we're ever divided, my destiny is death.

SHIP

This world is adorned in various ways.
I saw a strange contraption, an experienced traveller,
Grind against the gravel and move away screaming.
This strange creature could not see; it had no shoulders,
Arms, or hands; on one foot this oddity
Journeys most rapidly, far over
The rolling sea. It has many ribs,
And a mouth in its middle, most useful to men.
It carries food in plenty, yielding tribute to all people
Year by year, enjoyed by rich
And enjoyed by poor. Tell me if you can,
O man of wise words, what this creature is.

ANCHOR

I must fight with the waves whipped up by the wind,
Contending alone with their force combined, when I dive
To earth under the sea. My own country is unknown to me.
If I can stay still, I'm strong in the fray.
If not, their might is greater than mine:
They will break me in fragments and put me to flight,
Intending to plunder what I must protect.
I can foil them if my fins are not frail,
And the rocks hold firm against my force.
You know my nature, now guess my name.

ICEBERG

A curious, fair creature came floating on the waves,
Shouting out to the distant shores,
Resounding very loudly; her laughter was terrible
And fearsome to all. Sharp were her edges.
She is slow to join battle but severe in the fray,
Smashing great ships with savagery.
She binds them with baleful charm,
And speaks with characteristic cunning:
'My mother, one of the beloved maidens,
Is my daughter also, swollen and strong,
Known by all people as she falls on the earth,
Welcomed with love through the width of all lands.'

Note: The mother of the Iceberg is water, but since the Iceberg can melt
again, her daughter also is water.

ICE

On the way a miracle: water become bone.

FIRE

On earth there's a warrior of curious origin.
He's created, gleaming, by two dumb creatures
For the benefit of men. Foe bears him against foe
To inflict harm. Women often fetter him,
Strong as he is. If maidens and men
Care for him with due consideration
And feed him frequently, he'll faithfully obey them
And serve them well. Men succour him for the warmth
He offers in return; but this warrior will cruelly punish
Anyone who permits him to become too proud.

Note: The *two dumb creatures* are two flints, or pieces of steel, or even, possibly, two pieces of wood.

STORM AT SEA

Sometimes I plunge through the press of the waves
Unexpectedly, delving to the earth,
The ocean bed. The waters ferment,
Sea-horses foaming.
The whale-mere roars, fiercely rages,
Waves beat upon the shore; stones and sand,
Seaweed and saltspray, are savagely flung
Against the dunes when, wrestling
Far beneath the waves, I disturb the earth,
The vast depths of the sea. Nor can I escape
My ocean bed before he permits me who is my pilot
On every journey. Tell me, wise man:
Who separates me from the sea's embrace,
When the waters become quiet once more,
The waves calm which before had covered me?

SUN AND MOON

I saw a strange creature,
A bright ship of the air beautifully adorned,

Bearing away plunder between her horns,
Fetching it home from a foray.
She was minded to build a bower in her stronghold,
And construct it with cunning if she could do so.
But then a mighty creature appeared over the mountain
Whose face is familiar to all dwellers on earth;
He seized on his treasure and sent home the wanderer
Much against her will; she went westward
Harbouring hostility, hastening forth.
Dust lifted to heaven; dew fell on the earth,
Night fled hence; and no man knew
Thereafter, where that strange creature went.

Note: The *plunder* is the light the moon has captured from the sun in battle.

CREATION

I spread more wide than the bounds of the world,
I am smaller than a worm, outstrip the sun,
I shine more brightly than the moon. The swelling of the seas,
The fair face of the earth and all the green fields,
Are within my clasp. I cover the depths,
And plunge beneath hell; I ascend above heaven,
Highland of renown; I reach beyond
The boundaries of the land of blessed angels.
I fill far and wide
All the bounds of the earth and the ocean streams.
How can you tell me what is my name?

SWORD-RACK

I saw in the hall (where warriors were drinking)
A wondrous tree, of four timbers, brought
On to the floor; it was adorned with twisted gold
And with jewels inlaid most skilfully, and plated with silver —
A symbol of His Cross who for us

Established a ladder between Heaven and Earth
Before He harrowed Hell. I can easily
Tell you of *this* tree's origin:
The hard yew and the shining holly,
The maple and the oak serve their Lord
Together and together share one name —
An outlaw's tree it was that offered a weapon often
To its lord, a treasure in the hall,
The gold-hilted sword. Now tell me the answer
To this riddle, whoever will hazard
A guess as to what this tree is called.

Note: The Sword-Rack is in the shape of the Cross. It is made of four timbers, as the Cross was often said to have been. Once destined for the execution of outlaws, it is now adorned with gold, silver and jewels. This paradox is more fully developed in *The Dream of the Rood*.

BEAM

I am surrounded by flames and sport with the wind,
I am clothed with finery and the storm's great friend,
Ready to travel, but troubled by fire,
A glade in full bloom and a burning flame;
Friends often pass me from hand to hand,
And I am kissed by ladies and courteous men.
But when I raise myself, with reverence
Proud men must bow to me; I bring
Man's happiness to full maturity.

Note: The word *beam* in Old English had several different connotations, as revealed by this riddle. The meaning *Tree* suits lines 1b–2 and 3b–4a. It could also mean *Ship*, line 3a; *Log*, lines 1a and 4b; and *Cup*, lines 5–6 (or possibly *Harp*, line 5 and *Cup*, line 6). In lines 7–9, the riddle anticipates *The Dream of the Rood* in so far as it shows the Cross speaking in the first person.

THE CHARMS

'Of the numerous charms and exorcisms preserved in Anglo-Saxon manuscripts,' remarks Professor Dobbie, 'there are only twelve which are in metrical form or which contain verse passages of sufficient regularity to warrant their inclusion in an edition of Anglo-Saxon poetry.' Even some of these have quite large passages of prose, for example those for unfruitful land, for loss of cattle, for delayed birth, for the water-elf disease, and against a dwarf.

Our first reaction may be to smile tolerantly while we reflect how far beyond such childishness we have advanced. But have we? Are there no superstitions among pool-doers and horse-backers, among examinees and job-seekers, or among Mods and Rockers? I wonder. At times, I must admit, I have been tempted to say these two charms which won prizes in a 1948 *New Statesman* contest set by Naomi Lewis:

Charm for Obtaining Domestic Help

Sabaóth Zagoúre; Patoúre Eloaí.
  By these hidden names I speak,
  Woman, help us all the week.
  Ablathanalba hear my spell,
  Come on Saturdays as well.
  By the hidden names of power,
  Come for half-a-crown an hour.
O Soronophris Paphro: Baroúkh Adonaí Eloaí.

Charm for Getting Through the Customs

  Torkum chorkum pass me through,
  Search my bags without a clue,
  Catch the next man in the queue,
    Nihil declarare!
  Fijity fibity though I lie
  Take my word and let me by,
    In foro conscientiae —
    Nihil declarare.

Of the three charms here translated, the first two are primitive and pagan and are unaffected by Christianity. The third — *For Theft of*

Cattle — shows a blend of pagan and Christian which perhaps reflects the Church's willingness to baptize what it could not suppress.

CHARM AGAINST A WEN

For Dennis White with best wishes

Wen, wen, little wen,
Here you must neither build nor stay
But you must go north to the nearby hill
Where, poor wretch, you will find your brother.
He will lay a leaf at your head.
Under the paw of the wolf, under the eagle's wing,
Under the claw of the eagle, may you ever decline!
Shrivel like coal on the hearth!
Wizen like filth on the wall!
Waste away like water in the pail!
Become as small as a grain of linseed, and far smaller than a hand-worm's hip bone and so very small that you are at last nothing at all.

CHARM FOR A SWARM OF BEES

Concerning a swarm of bees. Take earth in your right hand, cast it under your right foot and say:
'I have it underfoot; I have found it.
Behold! Earth avails against all kinds of creatures,
It avails against malice and evil jealousy'
And against the mighty tongue of man.'

When they swarm, scatter earth over them and say:
'Alight, victorious women, alight on the earth!
Never turn wild and fly to the woods!
Be just as mindful of *my* benefit
As is every man of his food and his fatherland!'

CHARM FOR THEFT OF CATTLE

May nothing I own be stolen or concealed, any more than
Herod might steal or conceal our Lord. I thought of St.
Helena and I thought of Christ hanging on the Cross; thus I
attempt to find these cattle, not let them be carried off; to
hear word of them, not let them be injured; to have them
looked after, not let them be led away.

Garmund, God's servant,
Find those cattle and fetch those cattle,
Take charge of those cattle and guard those cattle
And bring those cattle home!
May that thief never own land to which he may lead them
    away!
May that rustler never own ground to which he may bear them
    off,
Or houses where he may hold my cattle as his own!
And if perchance he does, may it never profit him!
Within three nights may I know his strength,
His might and his power and his skill to protect!
May the man who plans to make off with these cattle,
Or desires to abduct them,
Wither away as dry wood withers!
May that thief be as frail as thistle! Amen.

THE RUIN

The Ruin tells of a deserted and ruined city with stone buildings — 'the old work of giants' — where there were once baths and hot springs. Hence it is tempting to identify it with Bath and some writers have done this. They may be right; while Professor Dobbie points out that Bath itself never seems to have been entirely deserted, the latest editor of *The Ruin* (Mr. R. F. Leslie) has shown that certain features in the description fit Bath and no other known site in Britain, and that the poet could therefore well be describing 'the scene as it must have appeared no later than the first half of the eighth century'. But it is possible that he was painting a composite picture incorporating features from several different places. Whatever the truth — and the point is not vital — he has succeeded in giving a fine general impression and some remarkably realistic detail, which is much more specific than that in the passages of *The Wanderer* which treat the same theme.

The poem has suffered as a result of the already-mentioned diagonal burn in the manuscript. But there is no reason for believing it contained any passages of philosophical or Christian reflection. The poet is aware that the most glorious objects must decay or disappear under the ravages of time and the elements, and that the bravest men must pass away as a result of disease or war — the latter seems to have been the subject of the damaged lines early in the poem. There is no mention of the fairest women and no suggestion that the poet is Christian or has any belief in an after-life for those who have passed away. These points are made clear by a comparison with the first two stanzas of a thirteenth-century poem on the theme *Ubi sunt qui ante nos fuerunt?*, presented here with the spelling modernized in places:

> Where be they before us weren,
> Houndes ledden and hawkes beren
> And hadden field and wood?
> The rich ladies in their bower
> That wereden gold in their tresour   *head-dress*
> With their bright rood;   *faces*

Eten and drunken and maden them glad;   [*They*]
Their life was all with gamen ilad,   *in pleasure spent*
Men kneeled them biforen,
They beren them wel swithe high —   *very proudly*
And in a twinkling of an eye
Their soules were forloren.   *lost*

Yet, unlike the author of *The Wanderer*, the poet does not break
into a series of 'Alas's'; in fact, he keeps himself out of the way. If
he is aware of the bullet, he bites on it bravely. There is no feeling of
self-pity and no suggestion that it was all wasted and not worth-
while. *Wyrd* the master has conquered as it must, but the men were
happy, the halls were bright, the city was a noble place.

THE RUIN

Wonderful is this wall of stone, wrecked by fate.
The city buildings crumble, the bold works of the giants decay.
Roofs have caved in, towers collapsed,
Barred gates are gone, gateways have gaping mouths, hoar
    frost clings to mortar.
Ceilings save nothing from the fury of storms, worn away,
    tottering,
Undermined by age. The earth's embrace,
Its clammy grip, has claimed the mighty craftsmen;
They are perished, gone. A hundred generations of men
Have passed away since then. This wall, grey with lichen
And red of hue, outlives kingdom after kingdom,
Weathers wild storms; the tall gate succumbed
But the wall itself still stands, hacked at by weapons . . .
    . . . .

The architect conceived a remarkable plan:
Ingenious and resolute, he bound the foundations
With metal rods into linking rings.
The city halls were beautiful, the bath-houses plentiful,
A wealth of gables stood in the sky; thunderous was the
    martial clamour;

F

All the many mead-halls overflowed with merriment.
But fate, inexorable, swept all this away.
Slaughtered men fell far and wide, plague tortured the town,
Death struck down every valiant man.
Their deserted ramparts became waste places,
The derelict city decayed. Its warriors and craftsmen
Lay dead in the earth. Thus these lordly courts are crumbling;
Over the redstone arch the roof framework
Is a skeleton, untiled. The ruins have tumbled to the plain,
Broken into craggy mounds of stone. Here, long ago, many a
    happy man
Was clothed resplendently in glowing gold.
Proud and flushed with wine, in his shining armour
He gazed upon his treasure . . . silver and curious stones,
Gold, gems, and precious jewels. . . .
And he gazed at this fine castle, too, built in a great kingdom.
Stone houses stood here, and a hot spring
Gushed from the earth in a swift stream.
The stone wall encompassed all,
The gaily painted baths ceaselessly supplied with steaming
    water.
The scalding water streams across the grey stones
Into the circular pool where the baths were . . .
        .   .   .   .
That city was a noble place.

DEOR

THIS is a more personal poem than *The Ruin* in that the poet tells us something about himself. According to the interpretation to which the conventional title *Deor* commits us, Deor is the name of a poet who has been the court *scop* or minstrel of the Heodenings for many years. Now he has been superseded by Heorrenda and has lost the land which is the minstrel's perquisite. In his misery he thinks of others who have suffered misery. But, he reflects, their misery passed over. He sees God's hand in this — there is no reason for accepting the view that such a Christian reference must be an interpolation — and is comforted by the reflection which runs as a refrain through the poem, that his misery too can pass away.

Scholars have found it hard to identify some of the people referred to by the poet and agreement has not been reached in all cases. In the comments which follow, the knot of controversy has been unceremoniously cut and one possible explanation has been adopted. Weland, the famous smith, was carried off by King Nithhad, hamstrung ('supple bonds of sinew'), and forced to serve as the royal smith. He wreaked a terrible vengeance by killing Nithhad's two sons and ravishing his daughter, Beadohild. After telling Nithhad what he had done, he escaped. Beadohild's child turned out to be a great hero. So both she and Weland passed through their troubles.

Nothing is known of Mæthhild and Geat, but the story can be taken as telling of two lovers separated by force of circumstances; compare *Wulf*, *The Wife's Lament*, and *The Husband's Message*. We must presume that Mæthhild and Geat were finally re-united. Theodric was apparently an exile from his own kingdom while ruling the Mærings. We do not know the reason for his exile or how his misery was alleviated. In the fourth stanza, it is the subjects of the Gothic tyrant Ermanarich who are unhappy as a result of his ruthlessness, not the king himself or any one individual sufferer. Things must have been bad when the warriors hoped for the overthrow of their king, for this was the worst of disloyalties.

Whether the Deor described by the poet is his real self or a *persona* through which he expresses a conventional *consolatio* is not clear.

Some, like the present translator, feel that the poem is intensely personal. Professor Dobbie, on the other hand, writes that

> though lyric and elegiac in form and mood, *Deor* belongs properly with *Widsith*, as a poem in autobiographical form, dealing with Old Germanic heroic material. And there seems to be no doubt that here, as in *Widsith*, the autobiographical element is purely fictitious, serving only as a pretext for the enumeration of the heroic stories.

We are not bound to accept this. But even if we do, it does not mean that the emotions are fictitious or the poem valueless.

The conventional interpretation outlined above has been followed in the translation. However, Mr. P. J. Frankis has recently put forward the suggestion that this poem and the one next translated — which alone among Old English poems have a stanzaic structure with a refrain — are

> dramatic monologues attached to the same heroic legend. In *Deor* we have the complaint of a warrior who was a *scop*, and this is evident in the style of his complaint; his sufferings are expressed indirectly by means of allusions to the traditional heroic legends that were the minstrel's stock in trade. [Mr. Frankis sees Theodric as a tyrant like Ermanarich.] In *Wulf and Eadwacer*, on the other hand, we have the complaint of a woman, and the style is accordingly direct and impassioned, without any reference to heroic legend. Thus the Anglo-Saxon poet gives us some measure of characterization in that the style of the complaint reflects the personality of the speaker.

Mr. Frankis gets over the difficulty that the man is called *Deor* in one poem and *Wulf* in the other by pointing out that the capital *D* is editorial and not in the manuscript, and by suggesting that *deor wæs min nama* (with the, for him, significant past tense) means 'my name was an animal' — *deor* is the modern word 'deer' which then meant 'any (wild) animal'. This would be a riddling reference to the name *Wulf*, to be compared with the use of the word 'song' for 'life' at the end of the next poem, which would be very appropriate if the man in the case were a minstrel. Mr. Frankis then reconstructs 'the approximate and, admittedly highly hypothetical, outlines of the story' illustrated by the two poems:

> Wulf is a warrior-minstrel at the court of the king of the Heodeningas; he loves the king's daughter (probably named Hild), and under the circumstances described in *Wulf and Eadwacer* 10–12, she conceives a child

by him; the king is enraged, and Wulf is forced to flee into exile; Heor-
renda receives Wulf's position at court, and also his estates; the king's
daughter is kept under guard on a remote island. The fate of the child is
not clear. . . .

He ends by suggesting the titles *First and Second Old English Refrain
Poems* instead of *Deor* and *Wulf and Eadwacer*, which (he rightly
points out) commit us to certain interpretations.

To adapt the translation given below to this perhaps too-ingenious
theory requires only a chance of 'Deor was my name' to 'My name
was an animal'. But Mr. Frankis sees the poem as giving, not a
'message of hope' but 'a statement of hopelessness, or at most a
message of merely stoical acceptance'. I am not sure that his theory
demands this view of *Deor* (though to be sure *Wulf* gives no vision of
joys to come), for the mention of the Lord seems to imply a
Christian interpretation. If we accept this, we shall find that the poet
— be he monk or Christian layman — offers us across the centuries
the distilled wisdom of his experience; as the psalmist says

> I have eaten ashes like bread, and
>   mingled my drink with weeping,
> Because of thine indignation and thy wrath:
>   for thou hast lifted me up, and cast me down.
> My days are like a shadow that declineth;
>   and I am withered like grass.
> But thou, O Lord, shalt endure for ever;
>   and thy remembrance unto all generations.
> Thou shalt arise, and have mercy. . . .

DEOR

Weland knew full well the meaning of exile;
That strong man suffered much;
Sorrow and longing stood him company,
And wintry exile; when *Nithhad*
Had fettered him, put supple bonds of sinew
Upon a better man, misfortunes beset him.
That passed away, this also may!

To *Beadohild*, her brothers' death was not
So great a cause for grief as her own state
When she realized she was
With child; she sank into despair
Whenever she thought what would come of it.
 That passed away, this also may!

Many of us have learned that *Geat's* love
For *Mæthhild* grew too great for human frame,
So that their grievous passion prevented them from sleeping.
 That passed away, this also may!

For thirty years *Theodric* ruled
The stronghold of the Mærings; that was known to many.
 That passed away, this also may!

We have heard of the wolfish mind
Of *Ermanarich*; a savage man,
He held wide sway in the kingdom of the Goths.
Many a warrior sat, full of sorrow
And expecting adversity, often wishing
That some foe would conquer his country.
 That passed away, this also may!

If a man sits in despair, deprived of all pleasure,
His mind moves upon sorrow; it seems to him
That there is no end to his share of hardship.
Then he should remember that the wise Lord
Often moves about this middle-earth:
To many he grants glory,
Certain fame, to some a sorrowful lot.
I will say this about myself,
That once I was a minstrel of the Heodeningas,
Dear to my lord. *Deor* was my name.
For many years I had an excellent office
And a gracious lord, until now *Heorrenda*,
A man skilled in song, has inherited the land
Once given to me by the guardian of men.
 That passed away, this also may!

WULF

THIS poem immediately precedes the first group of *Riddles* in the Exeter Book and was once thought to be a riddle itself. This view still commands a handful of supporters, but is no longer popular, for it is now generally agreed that the poem, like *The Wife's Lament*, is a dramatic monologue spoken by a woman separated from her lover. It will come as no surprise that Anglo-Saxon women loved their men, but we can be grateful for these variations on a universal theme. The title *Wulf* has been adopted instead of the more usual *Wulf and Eadwacer* or *Eadwacer* because all the theories seem to agree that a man named *Wulf* 'Wolf' is mentioned in the poem. This critical unanimity becomes less surprising when we find that the name occurs four (perhaps five) times. Unfortunately, agreement extends little further.

While the first line of the poem has not been satisfactorily explained, the basic difficulty is whether the word *eadwacer* is a proper name referring to a second man or whether it is a common noun meaning 'watchman of property, guardian'. Those who take the former view think that the poem describes an example of what we today call 'the eternal triangle' — a wife, a husband, and a lover. (We know nothing of such men or of the woman whose life was supposedly tangled with theirs, though, if this view is right, the story must have been well-known in its time.) Wulf is on one island. Eadwacer and the woman are on another. Some hold that Wulf is the lover and Eadwacer the husband, others the reverse. Who is the father of the child is not clear, although the word-play 'Wulf' — 'whelp' may suggest Wulf. Sick with longing for Wulf, the woman sits weeping. Eadwacer comforts her and she finds his embraces pleasant and yet distasteful. In her agony, she cries for 'Wulf, my Wulf'. Is her cry to Eadwacer a revelation to him that she has borne a child by Wulf whom Wulf will come to claim? Or has Wulf abducted Eadwacer's son? It is not clear. What is clear is her agony.

But others believe that there are only two protagonists — Wulf and the woman. If this is so, we have a situation parallel to that in *The Wife's Lament* — a woman lamenting the absence of her lover. This is the basis of Mr. Frankis's explanation. He suggests that 'the woman makes an equivocal reference to *eadwacer* (perhaps a personal name [referring to a guardian or to a man who betrayed the lovers], perhaps a noun meaning "watchman of property, guardian")'. A variation on this theme has been suggested by Mr. J. F. Adams who thinks that the word *eadwacer* is used ironically; Wulf is not the protector and guardian of the house. The irony of this lies, not in the fact that he is a wandering husband, but in the fact that the relationship lacks a binding religious or legal sanction. Wulf is a wanderer, perhaps a member of a band of sea-rovers. He is not married to the woman who loves him, but visits her spasmodically when opportunity arises. When he visits her, she feels ecstasy in the pleasure of the moment, but is miserable because she knows her happiness is fleeting. The sentence which Mr. Adams would translate 'A wolf will carry our whelp to the wood' is a pun on his name implying that some foe will carry the child off. Mr. Adams translates the last line 'Our bond is this riddle' and goes on: 'Their "marriage" illustrates a riddle ironical in its obviousness: things never joined are easily separated.' But an interpretation without ironical overtones can be obtained by translating *eadwacer* as 'guardian of (my) happiness.'

The translator has chosen to take Wulf as the lover, and Eadwacer as the husband, but there is no 'right' answer to the problem. The student of Old English meets difficulties of this kind because the poet often took for granted stories now lost. This is not to be wondered at. What is to be wondered at is the frequency with which, in spite of all the difficulties, the voice of the poet rings clearly across the centuries. We do not know who the woman was. But how poignant is her heart-rending cry 'Wulf, my Wulf'. How nearly it touches us all.

WULF

It is as if one gave a gift to my people.
Will they protect him if he is in peril?
    With us it is not so.
Wulf is on one island, I on another;
Marshes imprison that island;
Men live there who delight in cruelty.

Will they protect him if he is in peril?
   With us it is not so.
My thoughts journeyed far to join my *Wulf*;
When rain slapped the earth and I sat apart weeping,
When the brave warrior wound his arms about me,
I was filled with delight, yet also with despair.
Wulf, my *Wulf*, my yearnings for you
And your infrequent visits have made me ill;
I am sick from love, not of starvation.
Eadwacer, do you hear? *Wulf* will carry
Our miserable whelp to the wood.
How easily man can sever that which was never
Truly at one, the song of us two together.

THE WIFE'S LAMENT

THE interpretation offered below is that this poem, like the preceding one, is a dramatic monologue spoken by a woman separated from her lover. This is the popular view which has stood the test of time. There has been some argument about whether the lovers were actually married; this depends on the details of the interpretation we favour. Occasionally, however, the suggestion has been made that the speaker is an exiled and lordless warrior, and that the situation is akin to that in *The Wanderer*. This view has recently been put forward again. Its newest upholder says that the poem *Wulf* 'may be a feminine monologue but is too cryptic to be clearly intelligible'. Having thus disposed of that feminine monologue, he is able to argue that, if *The Wife's Lament is* a wife's lament, it is unique in Old English in that it speaks of love from a woman's point of view. Thus, he goes on, *The Wife's Lament* is much more likely to be spoken by a man. This desirable state of affairs is achieved by the simple device of changing three inflexional endings in the first two lines of the poem from feminine to masculine. And hey presto! we have a new poem *The Exile's Lament*. This is neither the time nor the place to refute this, though I believe such refutation possible. But the more usual view is followed here.

The situation which lies behind the poem is far from clear, and numerous interpretations have been put forward. That adopted here is the one recently advanced by Mr. R. F. Leslie in his edition of the poem. The woman has come from a foreign land to marry. She finds few friends and a husband who is involved in some sort of a feud and is meditating a crime. He tries to conceal this from her so that she will not share the guilt (lines 15–20). But he is discovered and exiled (lines 6–8). She tries to follow him, to take up again the service she as a retainer owes him, her lord — they are people of high rank (lines 9–10). But she is prevented by his kinsmen (lines 11–14). Thus the separation they have sworn to avoid is a reality (lines 21–26) and she is miserable because she is exiled from him (lines 7–10).

Now, in lines 27–41, she describes the conditions of life forced on her by his kinsmen. These griefs are the heavier ones mentioned in lines 1–5, in comparison with the absence of friends and the concern she felt for her husband when they were together (lines 15–20). Lines 42–53 have long been a difficulty; Mr. Leslie's valuable suggestion that the first three-and-a-half lines are a general reflection by which the woman tries to sustain her morale has been adopted here and some liberty has been taken in the translation to make the point clear.

This translation then adopts (as it is forced to do) one of a number of possible versions of the 'plot' of the poem. But the plot is not important. The poet has made us feel the anguish of the wife separated by exile from her husband without hope of re-union, and we hear her cry:

> How like a winter hath my absence been
> From thee. . . .

THE WIFE'S LAMENT

I draw these words from the well of my grief,
From the depths of my own sorrowful life.
I swear that in the years since I was born
I have never suffered such sadness as now.
I am tortured by the anguish of exile.

My husband forsook his family and lands,
Went down to the play of the tossing waves; I fretted
At dawn as to where in the world my lord could have gone.
Then I left home, set out as a solitary wanderer,
Hunting for the man whom to serve was all my happiness.
But kinsmen of my lord had laid careful plans
And schemed our separation, so that we should live
Most wretchedly, far from each other in this wide world;
I was seized with longings.

My lord had asked me to live with him here
Though I knew almost no-one in this, his land,
Found few loyal friends. Wherefore I am most miserable.

For I discovered my dear lord, whose outward face was
  gay,
Was troubled and tormented in his mind,
Dissembling and designing great injury.
How often we swore to each other
That nothing but death should ever divide us.
That is all changed now;
Our friendship is as if it had never been.
For ever and ever grief lingers with me;
For my loved one's feud with another man, I have to pay an
  unfair penalty.
My husband's kinsmen have forced me to live in a forest
  grove,
Under an oak tree in this earth cave.
This cavern is age-old; I am choked with longings.
Gloomy are the valleys, too high the hills,
Harsh strongholds overgrown with briars,
Joyless wasteland. The journey of my lord over the sea
Grips and paralyses me. There are so many lovers in this world,
Loving and beloved both in bed together,
When I in my loneliness dress before dawn
And climb to the oak tree from this cave-dwelling.
There I must sit through the long summer's day
And there I mourn my miseries,
My sad fate; for I am never able
To quiet the cares of my sorrowful mind,
Alleviate the longings that are now my life's lot.

But the young must strive to be serious of mind
And always stout-hearted; they must hide
Their heartaches, that host of constant sorrows,
Behind a smiling face.

                    My husband, too, is racked by grief.
Whether he now decides his own destiny, or whether he is
  banished
To a distant land — living under

Rocky storm-cliffs chilled with hoar-frost,
Weary in mind, surrounded by the sea
In some sad place — I know that he too
Is racked by grief; he remembers too often a happier home.
Grief goes side by side with those
Who suffer longing for a loved one.

THE HUSBAND'S MESSAGE

NINE poems come between *The Wife's Lament* and *The Husband's Message* in the Exeter Book, but the two are often taken together as involving the same pair of lovers. This is tempting because the idea of separation as the result of a feud may be read into both poems. It is true that certain words appear in both poems and that there are other similarities in situation. But the uncertainty of the man about his wife's response does not match the passionate fervour of the woman and the link remains only a sentimental possibility incapable of proof and capable of adding little to the poems even if it could be proved. It ceases to be even a possibility if we adopt some of the interpretations of *The Wife's Lament* outlined above. There is, of course, no guarantee that the situations portrayed were real ones, just as there is no doubt that the emotions evoked are genuine.

The general situation in *The Husband's Message* is that a messenger arrives from overseas bearing a message from a noble lord in exile to his wife. According to some, this messenger is actually a rune-stave, a piece of wood on which a message has been carved in runes, and the poem is the speech of this personified rune-stave. But Mr. R. F. Leslie has claimed in his edition of the poem that the terms the speaker 'uses of his master . . . indicate a lord and retainer relationship with which the limited and temporary nature of a rune-stave appears incompatible.' Moreover, he argues, the verb *sægde* 'said' (translated below 'With his own words he told me') 'is much more appropriate to a human messenger than to a rune-stave whose function is essentially the conveyance of a written message.' Mr. Leslie's suggestion is that the speaker is a human messenger and that the piece of wood serves as proof to the woman that the messenger is genuine. But some of the *Riddles*, *The Brussels Cross*, and *The Dream of the Rood*, can be cited as poems in which inanimate objects speak, and *The Husband's Message* may well belong to this genre of poetry. In the translation here presented, therefore, it is assumed that the speaker is a rune-stave, and the runes which appear in lines 49–50 of the poem have been left as they may have been intended by the poet — a secret shared only by the husband and wife.

For the rest, the poem can speak for itself. The husband and wife are of high rank. They have loved, sworn oaths of loyalty, and been separated by a feud. Now that the husband has carved out for himself a new life abroad and has achieved a position worthy of her and money enough to support her, he urges her to join him. The weather is right for sailing. All he asks of life, says the messenger, is the opportunity of showing that he is still faithful to the vows they once exchanged and still feels the same love he felt of old.

His love is more restrained than that of the woman in *The Wife's Lament*. Where she is racked by anguish and, in her passionate longing, puts love first, he seems a little calculating and perhaps unable to agree that 'love conquers all'. But it would be unjust to reproach him in Viola's words:

> We men may say more, swear more; but, indeed,
> Our shows are more than will; for still we prove
> Much in our vows, but little in our love.

For there is no escaping the quiet sincerity of his love for his wife, and no denying that he needs hers.

THE HUSBAND'S MESSAGE

Now that we're alone I can explain
The secret meaning of this stave. I was once a child.
But now one of the sons of men, living far from here,
Sends me on errands over the salt-streams,
Commands me to carry a cunningly-carved letter.
At my master's command I have often crossed the sea,
Sailed in the ship's hold to strange destinations.
And this time I have come especially
To sow assurance in your mind
About my lord's great love for you.
I swear that you will find in him
Great faith to you, great loyalty.

O lady adorned with such lovely ornaments,
He who carved the words in this wood
Bids me ask you to remember
The oaths you swore so long ago together;
In those distant days you lived in the same country,
Lived in love together,
Sharing one estate in the beautiful city.
Then a feud, a cruel vendetta, forced him to leave
This land of happy people; I was told to tell you,
Joyfully, that you should undertake a journey
Just as soon as you hear the cuckoo's sad song,
That mournful sound in the mountain woods.
After that, let no man delay you
Or stop you from sailing over the waves.
Go down to the sea, the home of the gull;
Sail south from here over the salt-streams
To the land where your lord waits in high expectations.
He nurses no greater wish in the world,
(With his own words he told me)
Than that both of you together, by the grace of God,
May give rings once again to men in the mead-hall;
Bestow gifts as before on companions
And warriors. He has won
Wealth enough, though he lives
Far away amongst a foreign people
In a beautiful land.
Forced by the feud to launch his boat from here,
He went over the waves alone in his youth,
Set forth on the way of the flood, eager to
Depart and divide the quiet waters. Now at last your lord
Leaves his sorrows behind him. He will lack nothing,
Neither horses, nor treasure, nor joy in the mead-hall,
O daughter of the prince,
He will want nothing else in the world
If only he may have *you* for his own,
Fulfilling the former vow between you.
I hear the runes S. and R.,

EA., W. and M. join in an oath
That he will wait for you in that country,
And will always love you for as long as he lives,
Faithful and true to your vows to each other,
The oaths you swore so long ago together.

CÆDMON'S HYMN

THE earliest text of *Cædmon's Hymn* which can be dated is that in the Moore Manuscript of Bede's *Ecclesiastical History*; it seems to have been written between 734 and 737. This, like the version in the Leningrad Manuscript of 746, is in Old English of the Northumbrian dialect. There are later versions in West-Saxon. The Hymn and the story surrounding it have given rise to much controversy. To rehearse the history of this would not be fruitful. For our purposes, the interest of the Hymn is three-fold.

First, there is the story of its singing as told by Bede. During the time when Hild was Abbess of Whitby (657–80), a figure appeared to the aged cow-herd Cædmon in a dream and urged him to 'sing creation'. To everybody's surprise, Cædmon sang this Hymn, although he had never before been able to sing. The abbess and her monks decided that the gift was from God. So passages of scripture were read to him by the monks and, after 'chewing his cud like a clean beast', he paraphrased these in verse. Even his teachers flocked to hear him.

Second, what is the significance of this? There is no doubt that the by-standers were surprised. The question 'Why?' is one of the points of controversy. The initial surprise was doubtless that Cædmon could sing at all. But this would have been only a nine-day wonder, and some explanation must be found for the continuing interest of the monks and learned men. A view which commands some acceptance is that their surprise was at the use of the pagan alliterative verse for Christian purposes, an accomplishment even more significant than that of Horace, who claimed that he was

> *princeps Aeolium carmen ad Italos*
> *deduxisse modos*
> 'the first to transplant Greek lyric measures
> to Italy.'

Someone or other must have done this for the first time. If we reject the view that it was Cædmon, as we are entitled to, we are merely left with an unknown. (It may have been another man of the same name, like the other William Shakespeare — the one who actually wrote the plays.) I prefer to believe the story and to think that the continuing interest was due, neither to the fact that Cædmon suddenly acquired the gift of song nor to the excellence of the song itself, but to the miracle by which Christian subjects were treated in heroic verse. For, as Professor Wrenn has remarked,

> If this poet was, in fact, the very first to apply the Germanic heroic poetic discipline of vocabulary, style, and general technique to Christian story and Christian edification, then, indeed, the *Hymn* must be regarded (as it must have been at the time of its original recitation) as a great document of poetic revolution in early Anglo-Saxon England. Whoever first applied pagan traditional poetic discipline to Christian matter set the whole tone and method of subsequent Anglo-Saxon poetry. He preserved for Christian art the great verbal inheritance of Germanic culture.

And this is the third point of interest for us. Cædmon set a fashion which later poets followed and which eventually gave us *The Dream of the Rood*, *Beowulf*, and *Piers Plowman*. Many of the phrases he used became stock formulae. I do not think he invented them; I fail to see how Christian missionaries in Anglo-Saxon England could hope to gain converts without having at their command such phrases as *ece Drihten* 'eternal Lord', *heofonrices Weard* 'Guardian of Heaven', and *Frea Ælmihtig* 'Almighty King'. But this great poetic measure was harnessed for Christian purposes because he obeyed the angel's command: 'Cædmon, sing me something.' No wonder that (as Bede reports) Hild and her monks agreed that 'the heavenly gift was given to him by God Himself' and that the Old English translator of Bede's *History* added the words *swa swa hit wæs* 'as indeed it was'.

CÆDMON'S HYMN

Now we must praise the Ruler of Heaven,
The might of the Lord and His purpose of mind,
The work of the Glorious Father; for He,
God Eternal, established each wonder,
He, Holy Creator, first fashioned the heavens
As a roof for the children of earth.
And then our guardian, the Everlasting Lord,
Adorned this middle-earth for men.
Praise the Almighty King of Heaven.

PHYSIOLOGUS

THE Old English *Bestiary* is based on the Greek and Latin *Bestiaries*, but contains only three poems. These represent a creature of the land (*The Panther*), of the sea (*The Whale*), and of the air (usually identified as *The Partridge*). But a leaf is missing in the manuscript and the last poem contains only some sixteen lines, so that the identity of the bird described is uncertain. This poem is not included here. But there are no good reasons for believing that other *Bestiary* poems have been lost from the Exeter Book.

The Panther opens with a general comment on the variety of God's creatures on land, sea, and air, and then proceeds to tell us of the Panther's characteristics — it has a beautiful coat of many colours, and is peaceable and well-disposed to all creatures except the Dragon. After feasting, it retires and sleeps for three days, arising refreshed. From its mouth comes a sweet perfume which inspires men and animals to follow it. This strange picture — in which, as Professor Kennedy rightly remarks, 'the Panther wears an air of medieval strangeness' — is not the product of Anglo-Saxon ignorance about the panther; it derives from the poet's sources. The poem then proceeds to elucidate the allegory and explains that the Panther is Christ, the Dragon the Devil, and the sweet fragrance the glorious news of the Resurrection. Professor Cook has pointed out that the Panther is used to represent Christ because in the Septuagint text of *Hosea* V:14 the word 'panther' appeared where the Authorized Version has 'lion' and 'young lion':

> For I will be unto Ephraim as a lion, and as a young lion to the house of Judah: I, even I, will tear and go away; I will take away, and none shall rescue him.

The Whale, with its vividly realistic description of the great sea-beast, is in this respect in marked contrast to *The Panther*. And while it follows the same formula, it uses it twice, describing two different characteristics of the Whale and giving two allegorical explanations. First, we are told how sailors mistake it for an island, and of their rude awakening as they plunge to a watery grave. (The great pioneer scholar Grein pointed out that the name *Fastitocalon* is a corruption

of the Greek name for the asp-turtle or shield-turtle which is the
disappearing island in earlier versions of the story — a monster
tortoise which was confused with the whale.) All this is very re-
miniscent of Milton's

> . . . or that Sea-beast
> *Leviathan*, which God of all his works
> Created hugest that swim th'Ocean stream:
> Him haply slumbring on the *Norway* foam
> The Pilot of some small night-founder'd Skiff,
> Deeming some Island, oft, as Sea-men tell,
> With fixed Anchor in his skaly rind
> Moors by his side under the Lee, while Night
> Invests the Sea, and wished Morn delayes.

This drowning of the sailors allegorizes the way in which Satan drags
men to Hell.

Secondly, the Whale, like the Panther, has a sweet breath. But he
uses it to attract fish into his mouth. When his mouth is full, he
snaps it closed and the fish are lost. So the Devil attracts men by the
sweet scent of sin and they too are lost.

Allegory is no longer a popular medium for religious instruction,
though a late thirteenth-century *Bestiary* of 802 lines survives. This
treats a dozen creatures, including a mermaid which, half-maiden
and half-fish, betokens hypocrites who are not what they seem. The
Old English versions of *The Panther* and *The Whale* are not without
their flashes of poetry. But it seems right to concede that their interest
for the modern reader lies rather in the way they illustrate now-
outmoded methods of presenting religious truths. In them, as in the
misericords of the Middle Ages, the realistic mingles with the fan-
tastic and the grotesque superstition illuminates the spiritual truth.

THE PANTHER

From here to the frontiers of this world
Are all kinds of curious creatures
Of which we'll never know the origin or number.
To the brink of the water which whirls round the earth . . .
The swing of the waves in the roaring sea . . .

Both birds and beasts are scattered,
Great multitudes moving over the earth.
I heard someone say strange things
About the nature of a certain beast
Well-known to men in far-off lands.
He has for his home, and holds as his domain,
The mountain caves. His name is Panther;
So say the sons of men about this solitary wanderer,
The men of wisdom in their writings.
He is always generous, and a firm friend
To one and all excepting the Dragon
With which, through all the devilry he can devise,
He at all times lives in fierce hostility.

The Panther is noble, gaily dressed
In every colour, just as men say . . .
Holy men . . . that Joseph's coat
Was dipped in every dye.
Every shade in Joseph's coat shone
More brilliantly than any other colour
Through the widths of the world;
Likewise the Panther's coat is more beautiful by far
Than the coat of any other beast,
With colours ever varying; each vies with the others,
In gleaming brightness growing,
To be called most fair of all.
The Panther's character is quite unique:
He is modest and meek, peaceful,
Loving and kind. He will not hurt or hinder anything at all,
Virulent only against the venomous Dragon,
His sworn adversary of whom I spoke before.
More than delighted with a good meal
He retires to his resting-place after the feast,
A remote corner in the mountain caves.
There the mighty warrior slumbers for three nights;
He settles down, falls sound asleep.
Then, gloriously invigorated after his rest,

He swiftly rises on the third day;
A sweet sound streams forth,
A harmonious melody from the beast's mouth.
And after the song a perfume issues
From that place, more pleasing,
Sweet and strong, than any flower or forest blossom,
More fragrant than the fair adornments of the earth.
Then from royal lodges and mead-hall benches
In many large towns, bands of hunting men,
Joined by the javelin throwers,
March along earth's paths with majesty and power.
And animals also do the same
When the song and the scent have swept over the earth.

So also does Lord God, the giver of joy,
Show kindness to all creatures
And to all men . . . except to the Dragon,
That author of evil. He is the aged fiend,
Consigned long ago to the cavern of tortures,
Fettered and confined in fiery chains.
But the Prince of Angels, the giver of victories,
Rose from the grave on the third day
After He had suffered death's torture for our sake.
And that was as a fragrance, enticing
And fair throughout the whole world.
Humble men hastened in their hundreds
From every side and quarter towards that scent,
From the sweeping plains that spread over the earth.
So spoke the wise Saint Paul:
'Without number through the widths of all the world
Are the gifts which God the Father,
The only hope of all his creatures,
Imparts to every one of us. He offers them with love,
To further our salvation.'
They yield a fine fragrance.

H

THE WHALE

And now I will speak about a certain kind of fish;
I will weave words with all my skill
About the mighty Whale.
Much to our despair, he is frequently found
To be savage and dangerous to seafaring men.
His name is *Fastitocalon*,
This floater of the ocean streams.
His form resembles some rough stone
Or clogged seaweed, tangled together
And beset by sandbanks, heaped in the water near the shore,
Inveigling sailors into supposing
Their straining eyes have caught sight of an island;
And then they secure the high-prowed ships,
Pay out the rope to this pretence land
And tie the sea-steeds at the water's edge.
The sailors disembark and intrepidly set out
To survey the land; the ships stand
Fast by the shore, surrounded by water.
At length the weary sailors set up camp,
Oblivious of all danger;
There on the island they kindle a fire,
Build up a high blaze; contented
But exhausted, they long to fall asleep.
As soon as the ocean monster, so highly skilled in treachery,
Surmises that the sailors are settled for the night
And rest in their encampment
Rejoicing in fair weather,
Then he sinks at once under the salt-wave;
To the extreme depths he plunges with his prey.
He delivers to be drowned in the hall of death
Both the ships and the sailors.

This is the method of evil spirits too,
The way of the devils who by dissembling

And by practising black magic betray man;
Inciting him to impair his good deeds
They lead him a dance wheresoever they will,
So that man ends by seeking solace from his enemies,
Deciding to settle down with the devils.
When the wily fiend feels absolutely sure
(That terrible creature from the torment of hell)
That man will come
To live within the limits of his jurisdiction,
He discloses a delight in dispatching him;
He kills that man with infinite cunning
Who has performed his will on earth in sinful pride
And wretchedness. Suddenly the devil, hidden by a magic
    helmet,
Dives down to hell with his unsuspecting victim,
That barren place, that bottomless swell
Beneath the misty gloom . . . just as the great Whale
Sinks under the waves with the sailors and ships.

The proud Whale, the water-traveller,
Has another habit even harder to believe.
When fierce hunger gnaws at him
And he feels a need for food,
The warden of the ocean opens his mouth,
Parts his wide lips. A pleasant scent
Streams out, and other kinds of fish
Are betrayed on this account:
They quickly swim to the source
Of the scent and all crowd in,
A thoughtless throng, until there is
Not an inch more room; and then those grim jaws
Suddenly snap, barring the way.

And such shall the fate be of any man
Who, in this fleeting life,
Has no control or care for his behaviour,
But lets himself be snared by the sweetness of a smell,

Some gross desire. He stands guilty
Before the King of Glory. The accursed devil
Opens the doors of hell after death
To those who ignore the true joys of the soul
And foolishly follow the false joys of the flesh.
When the malicious, wicked fiend
Has brought to the barren fen
And the whirlpool of fire
All who were ever attentive to his teaching,
Burdened with sins,
Then he firmly snaps his fierce jaws together,
Slams shut hell's doors after the slaughter.
For those who enter in, there is neither outlet nor escape,
There is not even a wisp of hope . . .
Any more than unfortunate fish in the sea
Can hope to escape from the Whale and swim free.
It is most surely for our good
That we should love the Lord of Lords,
Abandon the way of the devil in both word and deed
And go at last to see the King of Glory.
Let us always in this fleeting life
Strive towards peace and salvation,
So that we with the Beloved One
May enjoy Heaven in eternity.

THE WANDERER

The Wanderer tells the story of an exile. Once a member of a *comitatus*, he is now a lordless man alone with his memories. The hall lies ruined; its gold and silver is lost; its cups and benches are scattered; the comrades who drank with him and the lord who gave them gold are dead. He is left alone to think of

> departed joys,
> Departed never to return.

A reader who knows nothing more about *The Wanderer* will find that it gives him an insight into the exile's mind, and no inconsiderable poetic pleasure. There is much to be said for saying no more.

Yet more must be said, even at the risk of deserving A. E. Housman's famous stricture that 'works of this sort are little better than interruptions to our studies'. For, by the accident of time, we are left without any knowledge of what the author intended or of what beliefs he took for granted in his audience. Thus three vastly different views of *The Wanderer* exist, each with its own variations; they reveal the increasing sophistication of modern Anglo-Saxon literary criticism. The first is that *The Wanderer* was originally a pagan poem which was reworked by a Christian poet. This reworking may have consisted simply of adding the first five and the last four lines, which would mean that the original poem began and ended with lines starting *Swa cwæð* 'So spoke. . . .' The phrase *ælda Scyppend* 'shaper of men', which occurs about two thirds of the way through and which below is translated 'the Creator', presents some difficulties, but could be a pre-Christian expression surviving only here in its original pagan sense. There are other more complicated variations of this basic theory — which is by no means untenable. With such an interpretation the opening lines could be translated as a positive affirmation: 'Often the lonely Wanderer experiences the mercy and pity of God. . . .'

The second type of theory assumes that the poem is a unity written by a Christian poet describing the experiences of an individual. Some argue that the Wanderer is an imaginary figure through which the poet conveys his own views on life. Others claim that the poem represents the personal experience of the poet — a man who was once a warrior, but has found in Christianity a consolation which the heroic code failed to give. Professor Elliott has expounded this theory attractively. He sees the Wanderer as a warrior who has a guilty conscience because he did not die in the battle in which his lord was slain. Because of this, he has been unable to find a new lord and has been deprived of all that made his life as an heroic warrior worth living. But Christianity has brought forgiveness and comfort; the barrenness of his life in this world has been made more tolerable by the hope of Heaven. The poem is thus the story of the poet's life and spiritual development.

The third type of theory, which has been most fully expounded by Professor Smithers, sees the poem as a Christian allegory based on the familiar conception that life on earth is a pilgrimage towards Heaven and that those who live it are exiles from Heaven; as *The Epistle to the Hebrews* has it

> These all died in faith, not having received the promises, but having seen them afar off, and were persuaded of them, and embraced them, and confessed that they were strangers and pilgrims on the earth.
>
> For they that say such things declare plainly that they seek a country. . . .
>
> But now they desire a better country, that is, an heavenly: wherefore God is not ashamed to be called their God: for he hath prepared for them a city.

Along with this goes the commonly-held notion that the end of the world was imminent. If these verses from *Hebrews*, or something like them, preceded *The Wanderer* in the Exeter Book, this theory would presumably be right beyond peradventure. But, while the 'pilgrimage' theme is treated elsewhere in the Exeter Book (in the poem *Christ*), the allegory is there made explicit, as it is in *The Panther* and *The Whale*. The fact that there is no explanation of the allegory in *The Wanderer* is for some a strong argument against an allegorical interpretation. There are other difficulties too, such as the fact that some details of the poem do not readily fit the proposed allegory.

We are thus in a dilemma. Through no fault of the poem or the poet, we are left without an adequate frame of reference. We must therefore adopt that interpretation which appeals to us most or which the poem imposes on us. Whatever happens, we will (I think) find the poem worth reading. The problems which it treats are still real today. The emotions described are ones we have all felt.

The telling images of wind and winter, of cold and ice, of darkness, desolation and dawn-loneliness, the vivid evocation of ruined buildings, lost treasures, and dead comrades, and the poignant contrast with past joys, make us very aware of that

> Joy, whose hand is ever at his lips
> Bidding adieu.

Yet someone — it matters not whether it was the original poet or a later interpolator — found in all this, not despair, but hope, and passed his feeling on to us. And so those of us who are privileged to believe them realize afresh that the words of St. John the Divine apply with equal force to the Wanderer and his comrades and to us and our loved ones:

> Therefore are they before the throne of God, and serve him day and night in his temple: and he that sitteth on the throne shall dwell among them.
> They shall hunger no more, neither thirst any more; neither shall the sun light on them, nor any heat.
> For the Lamb which is in the midst of the throne shall feed them, and shall lead them unto living fountains of waters: and God shall wipe away all tears from their eyes.

THE WANDERER

The lonely wanderer prays often for compassion
And for mercy from Lord God; but for a long time
Destiny decrees that with a heavy heart he must dip
His oars into icy waters, working his passage over the sea.
He must follow the paths of exile. Fate is inexorable!

The wanderer's mind moved upon adversity
And savage slaughter and the ruin of kinsmen. He said,
'Time and again at the day's dawning
I must mourn all my afflictions alone.
There is no one still living to whom I dare open
The doors of my heart. I have no doubt
That it is a noble habit for a man
To bind fast all his heart's feelings with silence,
Whatever his impulse, his inclinations.

The weary in spirit cannot withstand fate;
Nothing comes of rankling resentment.
For this reason any man ambitious for renown
Confines his unhappiness to his own heart.
So ever since the day I covered my gold-friend
With dark clods of earth, I have had to keep
My thoughts to myself, and this despite my grief,
Cut off from free kinsmen, so far away
From my own dear country; for I left that land,
Ploughed the icy waves with winter in my heart;
In utter dejection I journeyed far and wide
Hunting for the hall of a generous gold-giver. . . .
For a man who would welcome me into his mead-hall,
Give me good cheer, (for I boasted no friends)
Entertain me with delights. He who has experienced it
Knows what a cruel companion sorrow can be
To any man who has few loyal friends.
For him are the ways of exile, in no wise twisted gold!
For him is a frozen body, in no wise the fruits of the earth!
He remembers hall-retainers and how in his youth
He had taken treasure from the hands of his gold-friend
After the feast. Those joys have all vanished.

A man who lacks advice for a long while
From his lord and friend lives thus in his loneliness:
In restless sleep he dreams that he clasps
And kisses his lord, and lays hands and head
Upon his lord's knee just as he had done
When he approached the gift-throne previously.
Then the lonely wanderer wakes again
And sees the dark waves surging around him,
The sea-birds bathing and spreading their feathers,
Snow flakes falling mingled with hail.

Then his wounds lie more heavy in his heart,
Aching for his lord. His sorrows are renewed;
The memory of kinsmen sweeps through his mind;

He welcomes them with songs, eagerly scans
His comrade warriors. Then they melt away again.
Their spirits do not bring many old songs
To his lips. Sorrow and care constantly
Attend the man who must send time and again
His weary heart over the frozen waves.

And thus I cannot understand why in the world
My mind is not tormented
When I brood on the fate of many brave warriors,
How they have suddenly had to leave the mead-hall,
The bold friends and followers. So it is this world
Day by day dwindles, and passes away;
For a man will not be wise until he has suffered
His share of winters in the world. A wise man must be patient,
Neither passionate nor hasty of speech,
Neither rash nor irresolute in battle;
He should not be timid, despairing, grasping,
And never eager to boast before he can implement it.
When it is his turn to boast a man must bide his time
Until he has no doubt in his brave heart
That he has resolved upon the right action.
A wise man must fathom how frightening it will be
When all the riches of the world stand waste,
As now in diverse places in this middle-earth
Old walls stand, tugged at by the winds
And hung with hoar-frost, buildings in decay.
The wine-halls crumble, heartbroken lords
Lie dead, all the proud followers
Have fallen by the wall. Battle laid claim to some,
Leading them on long journeys; the raven carried one
High over the waters, and one the grey wolf
Devoured; a warrior with downcast face
Hid yet another in an earth-cave.
Thus the Creator laid this world waste
Until the ancient works of the giants were deserted,
Hushed without the hubbub of milling inhabitants.

Then he who contemplates these noble ruins,
And who deeply ponders this dark life,
Wise in his mind, will often remember
The countless slaughters of the past and speak these words:
Where has the horse gone? Where the man? Where the giver
    of gold?
Where is the feasting-place? And where the pleasures of the
    hall?
I mourn the gleaming cup, the warrior in his corselet,
The glory of the prince. How time has passed away,
Darkened under the shadow of night even as if it had never
    been.
Where the beloved warriors were, there now stands a wall
Of miraculous height, carved with serpent forms.
The savage ash-spears, avid for slaughter,
Have claimed all the warriors — inexorable fate!
Storms crash against these rocky slopes;
Falling sleet and snow fetter the world;
Winter howls, then darkness draws on,
The night-shadow casts gloom and brings
Fierce hailstorms from the north to frighten men.
Nothing is ever easy in the kingdom of earth,
The world beneath the heavens is in the hands of fate.
Worldly possessions are ephemeral, friends pass away,
Here man is transient and kinsman transient,
The whole world becomes a wilderness.'

So spoke the wise man in his heart as he sat apart in secret
    thought.
He who is wise adheres to his beliefs; a brave man
Will not reveal the torments in his heart
Before he knows their remedy. It is best for a man to seek
Comfort and compassion from the Father in Heaven where we
    will all find security.

THE SEAFARER

THE similarity of style, thought, and emotion, between *The Wanderer* and *The Seafarer* is such that they are usually taken together, even though two poems separate them in the Exeter Book. The similarity extends to the basic theories; like *The Wanderer*, *The Seafarer* has been regarded in turn as a Christian adaptation of a heathen poem, as the experiences of a real or an imaginary human, and as an allegory of the soul's pilgrimage through life. But *The Seafarer* also has its own difficulties.

One which must be discussed is the part played by the sea. The first sixty-four-and-a-half lines of the poem show clearly the almost intolerable hardship of the seafaring life; when the sailor is at sea, he thinks with longing and envy of the joys which the land-dweller experiences. Yet when on land, he is driven to seek the sea. Why? We could understand it if we were told that the call of the sea itself drew the sailor irresistibly, despite all its hardships, for such a conflict in the mind of a man is easily understandable; as Catullus observed (of another kind of love, to be sure)

> *Odi et amo: quare id faciam, fortasse requiris.*
> *Nescio, sed fieri sentio et excrucior.*
>
> I hate and love. You ask how this may be?
> I only know its truth and agony.

But there is nothing in the poem to support this theory; if the first half stood alone, it would need some such title as 'The Seaman's Hard Lot' or 'Why Do I Go to Sea?'

Again, the fact that the sea is not mentioned after the first half of line 64 has led some to think that a later Christian poet was responsible for the second half of the poem. This view runs into the difficulty that the Lord has already been mentioned and that the first half of the poem seems to prepare us for a Christian conclusion. Other attempts have been made to divide the poem into pagan and Christian sections, but there is little agreement about where the divisions come between the original elegy and the later interpolations. Moreover, the dichotomy between pagan and Christian is, sometimes at least, artificial, for the theme of transience is common to both.

The theories which explain the poem as the work of one Christian poet describing the experiences of an individual are so many and varied that they cannot all be summarized here. Henry Sweet saw the poem as

> drawing a parallel between a seafarer's contempt for the luxuries of life on land on the one hand and the aspirations of a spiritual nature on the other, of which a sea-bird is to him the type. In dwelling on these ideals the poet loses sight of the seafarer and his half-heathen associations, and as inevitably rises to a contemplation of the cheering hopes of a future life afforded by Christianity.

For Professor Dorothy Whitelock the poem is a description of the life of a *peregrinus*, a man who sought eternal life by pilgrimage and permanent exile from his own land in this life. (Such men were not uncommon in Anglo-Saxon times; the Chronicle records the arrival at the court of King Alfred in 891 of three Scots — one called Macbeth — who had set out from Ireland in a skin boat without a rudder 'because they wanted to be in a foreign country, they cared not where, for love of God'.) According to this view the poem describes his actual experiences and elaborates the spiritual reasons which led him to adopt such a life. Others see both *The Seafarer* and *The Wanderer* as poems in which the universal theme of transience is handled by a Christian who uses a poetic tradition not yet fully reconciled to Christianity and yet affected by it; thus the poems can be taken at their face value as treating a real and personal theme by means of a conventional elegiac lament followed by Christian admonition.

The idea of life as a journey over a rough sea towards the heavenly harbour, which occurs several times in Anglo-Saxon homilies and poems, can be applied to *The Seafarer* to make it an allegory. This view has gained more support recently as a result of Professor Smithers's scholarly exposition of it. Yet the objections urged against such interpretations of *The Wanderer* — that elsewhere the allegory is made explicit and that some details of the poem do not fit the allegory — have also been made here. The latest editor of *The Seafarer* (Mrs. I. L. Gordon) sees the method of the poem as that of the medieval symbolic religious lyric rather than allegory; she writes

The reason why the emphasis has been on the sea-journey itself is revealed in lines 64b–66a, when the motive for the journey is made explicit. For at this point the 'life on land' becomes 'this dead, transitory life' (the worldly life of mortal man) which is 'dead' because it is less warm and living to him than 'the joys of the Lord'. In the light of this transformation the sea-journey becomes not only the personal act of one who prefers the difficulties and dangers of the sea to the comforts and pleasures of life on land, but also an act symbolic of the renunciation of worldly life generally and the ready acceptance of the struggles and sufferings involved in the quest for eternal bliss. And it is as a symbolic act that the Seafarer's journey serves as a bridge to the wider, more universal theme of the second half of the poem, which is a homily on the transitory nature of earthly prosperity and happiness and the importance of preparing for the life hereafter.

Each individual reader will have to decide for himself whether the poem is a unity. But it must be remembered that Anglo-Saxon ideas of unity may have differed from ours, and some of us find that, while *The Wanderer* and *The Seafarer* may lack the intellectual unity we demand, they treat a personal theme and offer us a unity of emotion and a poetical experience not to be despised. I have sufficient confidence in them as poems to believe that, despite all the difficulties, they will speak for themselves. Like the author of *The Seafarer*, the psalmist had actual sailors in mind in *Psalm* 107. But his words, like those of the Anglo-Saxon poet, have a wider significance:

Then they cry unto the LORD in their trouble, and he bringeth them out of their distresses.

He maketh the storm a calm, so that the waves thereof are still.

Then are they glad because they be quiet; so he bringeth them unto their desired haven.

O that men would praise the LORD for his goodness, and for his wonderful works to the children of men!

THE SEAFARER

I can sing a true song about myself,
Tell of my travels, of many hard times
Toiling day after day; I can describe
How I have harboured bitter sorrow in my heart
And often learned that ships are homes of sadness.

Wild were the waves when I took my turn,
The arduous night-watch, standing at the prow
While the boat tossed near the rocks. My feet
Were tortured by frost, fettered
In frozen chains; fierce anguish clutched
At my heart; passionate longings maddened
The mind of the sea-weary man. Prosperous men,
Living on land, do not begin to understand
How I, careworn and cut off from my kinsmen,
Have as an exile endured the winter
On the icy sea. . . .
Icicles hung round me; hail showers flew.
The only sound there, was of the sea booming —
The ice-cold wave — and at times the song of the swan.
The cry of the gannet was all my gladness,
The call of the curlew, not the laughter of men,
The mewing gull, not the sweetness of mead.
There, storms echoed off the rocky cliffs; the icy-feathered tern
Answered them; and often the eagle,
Dewy-winged, screeched overhead. No protector
Could console the cheerless man.

He who is accustomed to the comforts of life
And, proud and flushed with wine, suffers
Little hardship living in the city,
Will never know how I, heavy with weariness,
Have often had to make the ocean paths my home.
The night-shadow grew long, it snowed from the north,
Frost fettered the earth; hail, coldest of grain,
Battered the ground. But now my blood
Is stirred that I should make trial
Of the mountainous streams, the tossing salt waves;
My heart's longings always urge me
To undertake a journey, to visit the country
Of a foreign people far across the sea.
On earth there is no man so self-assured,
So generous with his gifts or so gallant in his youth,

So daring in his deeds or with such a gracious lord,
That he harbours no fears about his seafaring
As to what Almighty God will ordain for him.
He thinks not of the harp nor of receiving rings,
Not of rapture in a woman nor of any worldly joy,
But only of the rolling of the waves;
The seafarer will always feel longings.
The groves burst with blossom, towns become fair,
Meadows are beautiful once more, the whole world revives;
All these things urge the eager man
To set out on a journey over the salt streams.
And the cuckoo, too, harbinger of summer, sings
A mournful song, boding bitter sorrow
To the heart. Prosperous men know not
What hardship is endured by those
Who tread the paths of exile to the ends of the world.

Wherefore my heart leaps within me,
My mind roves with the waves
Over the whale's domain, it wanders far and wide
Across the face of the earth, returns again to me
Eager and unsatisfied; the solitary bird screams,
Irresistible, urging my heart to the whale's way
Over the stretch of the sea.
                                        So it is that the joys
Of the Lord inspire me more than this dead life,
Ephemeral here on earth. I have no faith
That the splendours of this earth will survive for ever.
There are three things which, until one
Occurs, are always unpredictable:
Illness or age or death in battle
Can deprive a doomed man of his life.
Wherefore each man should strive, before he leaves
This world, to win the praise of those living
After him. The best of posthumous fame
Is to achieve great deeds on earth
Against the malice of the fiends, against the devil,

So that the children of men may honour a man's name
And his fame at last may live with the angels
For ever and ever, in the joy of life eternal
Amongst the heavenly host.
                              Days of great glory
In the kingdom of earth are gone forever;
Kings and emperors and gold-giving lords
Are no longer as they used to be —
Once they wrought deeds of greatest renown,
Lived in most lordly splendour;
Such excellence proved ephemeral, those joys have passed
    away;
Weaklings thrive and hold sway in the world,
Enjoy it only through their own labours; all honour is laid
    low;
The earth's flower ages and withers
As now does every man throughout this middle-world:
Old age grasps his hand, his face grows pale,
Grey-haired he mourns; he knows that his former friends,
The sons of princes, have been placed in the earth.
Then, when he dies, his lifeless body
Cannot taste sweetness, feel the sharpness of pain,
Lift a hand or be lost in reveries of the mind.
Though a brother may bury his kinsman
Amongst the dead, strew his grave with gold
And the many treasures he wished to take with him,
The shining gold which a man stores on earth
Is of no assistance to his sinful soul
Confronted at the last by God's wrath.

Great is the fear of God; through Him the world turns.
He created the mighty plains,
The face of the earth and the sky above.
Foolish is he who fears not his Lord: death will find him
    unprepared.
Blessed is the humble man: he will find mercy in Heaven.
God gave man a soul to have faith in His great strength.

THE BRUSSELS CROSS

Two lines which will remind us of *The Dream of the Rood* are inscribed on a silver strip which runs round the edges of the Cross which now stands in the Cathedral of SS. Michel and Gudule in Brussels. The rest of the inscription is in prose and tells us that the two brothers Æthlmær and Athelwold had the Cross made to the glory of Christ for the soul of their brother, Ælfric. Elsewhere, we find the inscription 'Drahmal made me'. Who these men were and how the Cross got to Brussels is unknown. When it was made is also uncertain, but the language of the inscription suggests a date late in the tenth century or in the eleventh century. The most attractive theory is that the relic it contains is that 'part of the Rood on which Christ suffered' which the Anglo-Saxon Chronicle tells us Pope Marinus sent to King Alfred in 885 and that this relic passed out of the possession of Alfred's descendants towards the end of the tenth century. Its new owners then enclosed it in the present Cross and presented it to Westminster Abbey. Later, it was taken to the Continent, perhaps by Flemish soldiers in the time of King Stephen, and, after much wandering, ultimately found its way to Brussels.

Its past is therefore wrapped in mystery. But there is nothing mysterious about its message. The reversal of the traditional 'riddle' technique — it gives its name first instead of asking at the end 'What is my name?' — has seen to that. Not inappropriately, a new Church of the Holy Rood plans to have the first four words carved into the wall of the entrance porch:

Rōd is mīn nama.

THE BRUSSELS CROSS

Rood is my name. Once, trembling,
And wet with blood, I bore the Mighty King.

Æthlmær and his brother *Athelwold* had this cross made to the glory of Christ for the soul of their brother *Ælfric*.

THE DREAM OF THE ROOD

In *The Dream of the Rood* Christianity and the Germanic heroic code meet and are miraculously fused. After *Beowulf*, it is probably the outstanding poem in Old English, and — if that seems small praise to those who, despite the evidence, insist on thinking of the Anglo-Saxons as primitive people — it ranks with the greatest religious poems in English or any other tongue. The stark simplicity of its climactic phrase

Crīst wæs on rōde 'Christ was on (the) Rood'

sums up in four words the essence of the Christian faith.

The formal elements which make up *The Dream of the Rood* — the title is modern and misleading, for it is the poet, not the Cross, who dreams — can be paralleled in Old English literature. Constantine's vision of the Cross is treated in Cynewulf's *Elene*. The poet's 'I saw' and the Cross's 'I was' will be found in many of the Old English Riddles in this book, including two in which the Cross itself is mentioned — *The Sword Rack* and *The Beam*. Scholars will doubtless continue to argue whether the poem as here translated — *The Vercelli Book* version — was written at one time by one author, or whether those portions inscribed in runes on the eighth-century cross now standing in the church at Ruthwell, Dumfriesshire — which deal only with the Crucifixion — represent an earlier version to which a later poet added an account of the Resurrection and the Harrowing of Hell. The problem need not concern us. Similarly, it is immaterial whether the self-exculpation of the Cross is the poet's own contribution or is an example of the rhetorical device *purgatio*.

What is important is that *The Dream of the Rood* is firmly fixed in the Catholic tradition of the Veneration of the Cross. The two manifestations of the Cross may have been suggested by the plain blood-red Cross sometimes then used on Good Friday and by the jewelled Cross of Easter Day. It seems likely that the poet knew the Holy Week Liturgy, especially the Good Friday Adoration of the Cross and the Latin hymns of Venantius Fortunatus *Vexilla Regis* and *Pange Lingua* (to be found in *Hymns Ancient and Modern* as 'The Royal Banners forward go' and 'Sing, my tongue, the glorious battle'). The following parallels are of particular interest, though they are cited to demonstrate an attitude of mind and spirit, not for the sake of parading verbal resemblances:

(i) From the Liturgy itself, the cry

Behold the wood of the Cross, on which hung the Saviour of the World: come, let us adore

and the antiphon

We adore Thy Cross, O Lord: and we praise and glorify Thy Holy Resurrection: for by the wood of the Cross the whole world is filled with joy;

(ii) From the *Vexilla Regis*

God reigned from the Tree,

O Tree of glory, Tree most fair,
Ordain'd those Holy limbs to bear,
How bright in purple robe it stood,
The purple of a Saviour's Blood,

and

Hail, Cross, thou only hope of men;

(iii) From the *Pange Lingua*, the anthropomorphization of the Cross seen in the verses

Bend, O lofty Tree, thy branches,
Thy too rigid sinews bend;
And awhile the stubborn hardness,
Which thy birth bestow'd, suspend;
And the Limbs of Heaven's high Monarch
Gently on thine arms extend.

Thou alone wast counted worthy
This world's ransom to sustain
That a shipwreck'd race for ever
Might a port of refuge gain,
With the sacred Blood anointed
Of the Lamb for sinners slain.

Numerous other echoes of the teaching of the Church in those days could be cited, but one more must suffice. The Cross's comparison of itself with Mary suggests that both were Virgin instruments

I

in the service of our Lord. That this is no far-fetched idea is shown by the fact that Ælfric later saw the Tomb in the same role:

> It was right that a new tomb which had received no other should be found, just as Mary, Christ's Mother, was Virgin and mother, and bore no other.

Compare with this the observation of the Dean of Westminster, Dr. Eric Abbott, that 'the grave of Jesus is a *life-giving tomb*, a tomb which is the very womb of everlasting life for a redeemed mankind'.

It is clear from the *Vexilla Regis* phrase 'God reigned from the Tree' and from the idea in the *Pange Lingua* of the Crucifixion as a 'glorious battle' in which the Cross was 'the Victor's trophy', that the concept of Christ as a Warrior-King offering Himself as a voluntary sacrifice was not a Germanic invention. Yet it is a concept which must have appealed to a people who put such value on ferocious courage and pride and who lived according to the *comitatus* code in which the lord was the ring-giver and great hero for whom his warriors were duty-bound to die loyally and without complaint. In *The Dream of the Rood* all the world laments Christ's death and therefore forms His *comitatus*. But two members of His warrior-band are particularly singled out — the Cross and the dreamer. The irony of the Cross's situation as a retainer could not conceivably have escaped an Anglo-Saxon audience, to whom disloyalty to one's lord — whether by deserting him in battle, by failing to avenge him, or by killing him — was the worst of crimes. For the Cross, Christ's retainer, does not stand a passive spectator at his Lord's death. That would be bad enough. He is the agent of that death. Yet, in that hour of supreme disloyalty, the Cross is most loyal and obedient to his Lord's command. And, by a further paradox, he is a conscripted volunteer. He did not want to crucify Christ. But he did want to do his Lord's will. So he had to stand firm of his own free-will.

The poem is a dramatic account of a mystical experience in which the dreamer hears the Cross give a vivid first-person confession of his part in the Crucifixion. The Cross speaks of himself in the third person only twice (lines 40 and 56), when the first person would have been bathetic. He speaks only of things within his own experience. Hence there is no mention of Gethsemane, and the emphasis is on the agony of the Cross — for it was natural for the Cross to

speak of what he himself felt. But Christ's agony is not neglected —
'I saw the God of Hosts stretched on the rack' — and the two suffer
together (line 48). Though there is tension between the human and
divine aspects, the suggestion that Christ's Humanity is represented
in the passive enduring Cross and His Divinity in His own triumph
as the heroic victorious warrior should not be pressed too far. Both
undergo willingly an experience they would fain avoid and both
share the suffering and the triumph.

But, being a Christian, the poet does not stop at the Crucifixion;
for him, the alleged artistic inferiority of the second half would be
an irrelevant objection, the inevitable consequence of man's in-
ability to portray the ineffable. Like Salvador Dali in his painting
Christ of St. John of the Cross, he has given us an original and evoca-
tive vision of the Crucifixion and like him he moves on to show its
significance for the individual and for the world. The Cross and
Christ have been identified in suffering; the Cross is nailed with
Christ and Christ's blood flows on him. But the identification does
not stop there. After being crucified with Christ, the Cross is buried
with Him, and raised with Him. Once red and covered with blood
as an agent of the Crucifixion, then buried in the darkness of the
tomb, the Cross now shines in glory as an agent of our Salvation.
And in a marvellous way, the dreamer shares these experiences.
Once stained with sins — those sins in which he crucified to himself
the Son of God afresh (see *Hebrews* VI:6 and the Reproaches of the
Good Friday Liturgy) — he now looks forward to the day when he
will find the bliss of Heaven. Once, like the Cross, an agent in the
Crucifixion, he becomes like the Cross an agent in our Salvation
through this poem. So too the man he once was has been crucified
with Christ (*Romans* VI:6), has been buried with Him in baptism, and
has risen with Him through faith in the power of God who raised
Him from the dead (*Romans* VI:4 and *Colossians* II:12). And we
share the dreamer's experience — we who crucify the Lord daily by
our sins are crucified with Him, are buried with Him, and rise with
Him, with our eyes on the Heaven we cannot earn but dare to hope
for through His mercy and goodness. For this great mystery and for
this poem which expresses it so magnificently, we should surely
say

Deo gratias 'Thanks be to God.'

THE DREAM OF THE ROOD

Listen! I will describe the best of dreams
Which I dreamt in the middle of the night
When, far and wide, all men slept.
I perceived a strange and lovely tree,
Most radiant, rising up before me
Surrounded by light; it was clothed
In gleaming gold; five precious jewels
Studded its cross-beam and many more were strewn
Around it on the earth. All the angels of the Lord protected it,
Created so fair. That was no cross of a malefactor,
But holy spirits and men of this earth
Watched over it there . . . the entire universe.

This Cross of victory was so pure, and I was stained
With the black of sin. I saw this beautiful tree
Gloriously dressed and gleaming with gold; jewels rightfully
Adorned the tree of my Lord.
Yet I could see signs through that gold
Of malicious deeds of wretched men, that once dark blood
    had fled
Down the right hand side. Then I bowed deep in sorrow,
Frightened at this sight; I saw that sign frequently change
Its clothing and hue . . . at times bedewed with moisture,
Stained by flowing blood, at times bejewelled with gems and
    glittering gold.
I lay there for a long while
Gazing sadly at the Saviour's Cross
Until I heard it utter words;
The finest of trees began to talk:
'I remember the morning a long time ago
That I was felled at the edge of the forest
And severed from my roots. Strong enemies seized me
And fashioned me for their sport, bade me hold up their
    felons on high.

They shifted me on their shoulders and set me down on a
    hill.
It took many men to fasten me there. I saw the Lord of Mankind
Courageously hasten to climb upon me.
O then I dared not bend or break
Against the wish of my Lord, though the surface
Of the earth trembled with fear. I could have felled
All my foes, yet I stood firm.
Then the young warrior, God our Saviour,
Valiantly stripped before the battle; with courage and resolve,
Beheld by many, He climbed upon the Cross to redeem Man-
    kind.
I quivered when the hero clasped me; yet I dared not bend
    down to the earth,
Or fall flat in the dust. I had to stand firm.
A rood was I raised up; I bore aloft the mighty King
The Lord of Heaven. I dared not stoop.
They drove dark nails into me; dire wounds are there to see,
The gaping gashes of malice; I did not dare retaliate.
They insulted both of us together; I was drenched in the
    blood
That streamed from the side of the Man, when He had set His
    spirit free.

'High on the hill I suffered
Such grief; I saw the God of Hosts
Stretched on the rack; darkness blacker than night
Covered the radiant corpse of the Lord.
Shadows swept across the land,
Dark shapes under the low flying clouds. All creation wept,
Wailed for the death of the King; Christ was on the Cross.
Nevertheless from near and from far noble men came
To the solitary Prince; I saw all that too.
I was pierced with pain, yet I humbly bowed to the hands of
    men
Most readily. There they released Him from His heavy
    torment,

They took Almighty God away. The warriors left me standing there

Stained with blood; sorely was I wounded by the sharpness of spear-shafts.

They laid Him down, weary of limb, and watched over Him;

They looked at the Lord of Heaven there, as He lay resting for a while,

Weary after battle. And then they began to build a sepulchre;

Unconcealed from the eyes of his murderers, they carved it out of the gleaming stone.

Therein they laid the Lord of Victories. Then before they departed

At the end of that sad evening, they lamented in deep sorrow

For their glorious Prince; He rested in the grave alone.

But we still stood there, weeping blood,

Long after the song of the warriors

Had soared to Heaven; the Corpse grew cold,

The fair human house of the soul. Then our enemies hastened

To fell us by night; that was a terrible fate!

They threw us into a pit dug out and prepared as our grave;

But the friends of the Lord discovered me there,

And girded me with gold and shimmering silver.

'So, my dear friend, you have heard me describe

How I endured such anguish

And the bitterness of pain. But the time is now come

When men far and wide through the widths of the world . . .

And all this bright creation . . . bow down before me.

They pray to this sign. On me the Son of God

Suffered for a time; wherefore I now stand on high,

Gleaming under Heaven; and I have the power to heal

All those who revere me.

A long time ago I was torturer,

Hated by men, until I opened

To them the true way of life.

Lo! The Lord of Heaven, the Prince of Glory,

Showed preference for me over any other tree in the wood
Just as He, the Lord God Almighty,
Put His own mother, Mary,
Before all other women in the world.
Now I command you, my dear friend,
To describe your dream to other men.
Go and tell them that I am the Tree of Glory
On which the Son of God suffered for a while,
So as to redeem the sins of all mankind
And atone for Adam's wickedness.
He sipped the drink of death. Yet He rose again,
Determined with His strength to deliver man.
He ascended into Heaven. Almighty God, with all His host of
    angels,
Will descend to this middle-world again
On Domesday, to reckon with each man;
He will pronounce judgement — and has the power to do
    so —
On every single person, just as he deserves
For the way in which he lived this transitory life.
No-one then will be able to ignore
The well-weighted words spoken by the Lord.
He will ask of each man whether he,
In God's name, would undergo the pangs of death,
Just as He had done Himself upon the Cross.
And men will be caught in the clutches of terror
Giving scant thought to what they say to Christ.
But no-one need be numbed by fear
Who carries the best of all signs in his breast;
Each soul that has longings to live with the Lord
Must search for a kingdom far beyond the frontiers of this
    world.'

Then in wonder and joy I worshipped the Cross
Most willingly, although I was alone
With my own poor company. My soul was
Inspired to prepare for a journey. I sensed great yearnings

Surging up within me. The last years of my life
Will be leavened with joy, for I can turn
More frequently than any other man to that Tree of Victory,
And tender my devotion. These dear longings
Master my heart and mind . . . my help derives
From Holy Cross itself. I have not
Many friends of influence here on earth; they have journeyed
    on
From the joys of this world to find the King of Glory,
Gone hence to Heaven to live with God the Father
In eternal splendour. Now I look day by day
For that time when the Cross
Which once I saw in a dream here on earth
Will fetch me away from this fleeting life
And lift me to the home of happiness . . .
To the heights of Heaven, where the people of God
Are seated at the feast in eternal bliss;
I bide that time when the Cross will set me down
At the source-spring of glory to share
The happiness of the saints. I pray that the mighty Son of God,
Who once suffered agony on that tree of shame
For me and for all men, may always be my friend,
He has redeemed us; He has given life to us,
And a home in Heaven.

THE DREAM OF THE ROOD, lines 39–56.

'A living dog is better than a dead lion' observed the Preacher; it is in this belief that these translations are offered. However, in the hope that some idea of the majesty of the living lion can be transmitted to those not privileged to see him, an extract from *The Dream of the Rood* is printed below in the original from Sweet's *Anglo-Saxon Reader*, together with a literal gloss and some simple instructions for reading it. It is hoped that the attempt will not be thought a mere travesty akin to stripping a lion of his dignity by forcing him to jump through a circus hoop. It is offered sincerely, with the aim of giving some understanding and some pleasure.

Old English Text

Onġyrede hine þā ġeong hæleð,   þæt wæs God ælmihtiġ,
strang and stīðmōd;   ġestāh hē on ġealgan hēanne
mōdiġ on manigra ġesyhðe,   þā hē wolde mancyn lȳsan.
Bifode iċ þā mē se beorn ymbclypte: ne dorste iċ hwæðre
     būgan tō eorðan,
feallan tō foldan scēatum,   ac iċ sceolde fæste standan.
Rōd wæs iċ ārǣred,   āhōf iċ rīċne cyning,
heofona hlāford,   hyldan mē ne dorste.
Þurhdrifan hī mē mid deorcan næġlum,   on mē syndon þā
     dolg ġesīene,
opene inwidhlemmas: ne dorste iċ hira æniġum sceððan.
Bysmeredon hīe unc būtū ætgædere;   eall iċ wæs mid blōde
     bestēmed,
begoten of þæs guman sīdan,   siððan hē hæfde his gāst
     onsended.
Feala iċ on þām beorge   ġebiden hæbbe
wrāðra wyrda: ġeseah iċ weruda God
þearle þenian: þystro hæfdon
bewrigen mid wolcnum   Wealdendes hrǣw,
scīrne scīman   sceadu forðēode,
wann under wolcnum.   Wēop eal ġesceaft,
cwīðdon cyninges fyll: Crīst wæs on rōde.

Reading Instructions

(i) Read slowly, pausing between half-lines according to the punctuation.

(ii) Follow generally the stress and intonation of Modern English. There are usually two main stresses in each half-line, one of which must fall on an alliterating syllable.

(iii) Vowels

     a and *ā* as in 'aha' respectively.

     æ and *ǣ* as in 'mat' and 'has' respectively.

     e, i, o as in Modern English.

     u as in 'pull' (NOT 'hut').

     ē as in 'hate'.

     ī as in 'seen'.

     ō as in 'goad'.

     ū as in 'cool'.

     y and *ȳ* as *i* and *ī*, with lips in a whistling position. (Cf. Modern French *tu* and *ruse* respectively.)

Literal Gloss

Ungeared him(self) then (the) young hero, that was God almighty,
strong and firm-minded; climbed he on gallows high
brave in sight of many, because he would mankind release.
Trembled I when me the warrior embraced: not dared I however
    bow to earth,
fall to (the) land's surface, but I had fast to stand.
Rood was I reared (up), lifted I (the) powerful king
Heaven's lord, to bow myself not dared.
Through-drove they me with dark nails, on me are the wounds
    visible,
open malice-strokes: not dared I any of them hurt.
Insulted they us both together; all I was with blood
    be-steamed,
poured from the man's side, after he had his ghost on-sent.
Much I on the mount endured have
of cruel experiences: saw I (the) God of Hosts
cruelly stretched: darkness had
veiled with clouds (the) Ruler's corpse,
(the) bright radiance (a) shadow oppressed,
dark under clouds. Wept all creation
lamented (the) King's fall: Christ was on Rood.

Vowels in unstressed syllables should be pronounced clearly. This includes
vowels at the end of words.

(iv) Diphthongs
    ea, eo, ie and *ēa, ēo, īe* may be pronounced as written.
    But they are diphthongs, like the word 'I', not two vowels like *ea* in
'Leander'.

(v) Consonants
    All consonants are pronounced. Double consonants are pronounced twice.
þ and ð = *th*.
    Most of the consonants are pronounced as they are today. The main ex-
ceptions are:
    c = *k*.
    ċ like *ch* in 'child'.
    ġ like *y* in 'yet'.
    h at the beginning of a word as in 'hound'.
    h otherwise like German *ch*.
    sc like *sh* in 'ship'.

FURTHER READING

Editions of the Poems

All extant Old English poetry can be found in Volumes I–VI of *The Anglo-Saxon Poetic Records* (Columbia University Press and Routledge and Kegan Paul).

Standard editions of the poems translated here are:

The Battle of Maldon, ed. E. V. Gordon (Methuen, 1937: 2nd ed., 1949)

The Battle of Brunanburh, ed. A. Campbell (Heinemann, 1938)

The Finnesburh Fragment. See the editions of *Beowulf* described below

The Riddles of the Exeter Book, ed. F. Tupper, Jr. (Ginn, 1910)

Old English Riddles, ed. A. J. Wyatt (Heath, 1912)

Anglo-Saxon Charms, ed. F. Grendon (Steckert, New York, 1930)

Wulf. See the editions of *The Riddles* described above

Deor, ed. Kemp Malone (Methuen, 1933: 2nd ed., 1949)

The Ruin, The Wife's Lament and *The Husband's Message* are all included in *Three Old English Elegies*, ed. R. F. Leslie (Manchester University Press, 1961)

For *Cædmon's Hymn*, see *Three Northumbrian Poems*, ed. A. H. Smith (Methuen, 1933)

The Panther and *The Whale* will be found in *The Old English Physiologus*, ed. A. S. Cook (Yale Studies in English LXIII, 1921)

For *The Wanderer*, see *Anglo-Saxon and Norse Poems*, ed. and trans. by N. Kershaw (C.U.P., 1922)

The Seafarer, ed. I. L. Gordon (Methuen, 1960)

The Dream of the Rood, ed. Bruce Dickins and Alan S. C. Ross (Methuen, 1934: 3rd ed., 1951)

For *Beowulf*, see

Beowulf and the Fight at Finnsburg, ed. Fr. Klaeber (Heath: 3rd ed., 1941 or later)

Beowulf with the Finnesburg Fragment, ed. C. L. Wrenn (Harrap, 1953)

Translations

For a prose translation of *Beowulf,* see *Beowulf and the Finnesburg Fragment,* trans. by J. R. Clark Hall and C. L. Wrenn (George Allen and Unwin, 1950).

There is a verse translation by Gavin Bone — *Beowulf* in modern verse with an essay and pictures (Oxford, 1945).

Prose translations of many of the remaining poems will be found in *The Cædmon Poems,* trans. by C. W. Kennedy (Routledge, 1916) and *The Poems of Cynewulf,* trans. by C. W. Kennedy (Peter Smith, 1949).

A selection of the religious poetry, translated into alliterative verse, will be found in *Early English Christian Poetry,* trans. by C. W. Kennedy (Hollis and Carter, 1952).

Bibliography and Criticism

W. L. Renwick and H. Orton, *The Beginnings of English Literature to Skelton 1509* (Cresset Press: 2nd ed., 1952)

W. P. Ker, *Medieval English Literature* (O.U.P., 1912)
The Dark Ages (Nelson, 1955)

C. W. Kennedy, *The Earliest English Poetry* (O.U.P., 1943)

J. R. R. Tolkien, *Beowulf, The Monsters and The Critics* (British Academy Lecture, 1936)

D. Whitelock, *The Audience of Beowulf* (Clarendon Press, 1951)

Alan Bliss, 'v. The Appreciation of Old English Poetry' in *An Introduction to Old English Metre* (Basil Blackwell, Oxford, 1962)

C. L. Wrenn, '7. Verse-Technique' in *Beowulf with the Finnesburg Fragment* (Harrap, 1953)

H. C. Wyld, 'Diction and Imagery in Anglo-Saxon Poetry', Essays and Studies XI (1925), 49–91

D. C. Collins, 'Kenning in Anglo-Saxon Poetry', Essays and Studies XII (1959), 1–17

L. D. Lerner, 'Colour Words in Anglo-Saxon', Modern Language Review XLVI (1951), 246–9

F. P. Magoun Jr., 'Oral-Formulaic Character of Anglo-Saxon Narrative Poetry', Speculum XXVIII (1953), 446–467

Detailed Interpretations of Individual Poems

The following articles have been referred to:

P. J. Frankis, '*Deor* and *Wulf and Eadwacer*: Some Conjectures', Medium Ævum XXXI (1962), 161–175

J. F. Adams, '*Wulf and Eadwacer*: an Interpretation', Modern Language Notes LXXIII (1958), 1–5

R. C. Bambas, 'Another View of the Old English *Wife's Lament*', Journal of English and Germanic Philology LXII (1963), 303–9

R. W. V. Elliott, 'The Wanderer's Conscience', English Studies XXXIX (1958), 193–200

G. V. Smithers, 'The Meaning of *The Wanderer* and *The Seafarer*', Medium Ævum XXVI (1957), 137–153

I. L. Gordon, 'Traditional Themes in *The Wanderer* and *The Seafarer*', Review of English Studies V (1954), 1–13

D. Whitelock 'The Interpretation of *The Seafarer*' in *The Early Cultures of North-West Europe: H. M. Chadwick Memorial Studies* (Cambridge, 1950), pp. 261–72

Metre

Professor J. R. R. Tolkien has explained Old English metre in terms of Modern English examples in C. L. Wrenn's revision of J. R. Clark Hall's translation of *Beowulf* (George Allen and Unwin, 1950), pp. xxviii–xliii. Professor C. L. Wrenn discusses metre briefly in his edition of *Beowulf with the Finnesburg Fragment* (Harrap, 1953), pp. 77–80. See also Alan Bliss, *An Introduction to Old English Metre* (Basil Blackwell, Oxford, 1962).

Learning Old English

Anyone inspired to learn Old English as a result of reading this book will find a primer especially prepared for the beginner in *A Guide to Old English* by Bruce Mitchell (Basil Blackwell, Oxford, 1965). It can be used by those working without a teacher.

Note: It is hoped that Professor C. L. Wrenn's book, *Anglo-Saxon Literature*, to be published by Harrap, will appear in 1965.

Printed in Great Britain
by Richard Clay (The Chaucer Press), Ltd.,
Bungay, Suffolk.